The Dangers of Synthetic Drugs

Carla Mooney

ReferencePoint Press®

San Diego, CA

© 2017 ReferencePoint Press, Inc.
Printed in the United States

For more information, contact:
ReferencePoint Press, Inc.
PO Box 27779
San Diego, CA 92198
www.ReferencePointPress.com

LIBRARY OF CONGRESS CATALOGING-IN-PUBLICATION DATA

Names: Mooney, Carla, 1970- author.
Title: The dangers of synthetic drugs / by Carla Mooney.
Description: San Diego, CA : ReferencePoint Press, Inc., 2017. | Series: Drug
  dangers | Includes bibliographical references and index.
Identifiers: LCCN 2016007725 | ISBN 9781682820261 (hardback)
Subjects: LCSH: Designer drugs--Juvenile literature. | Synthetic
drugs--Juvenile literature. | Drug abuse--Juvenile literature.
Classification: LCC RM316 .M66 2017 | DDC 615.3/1--dc23 LC record
available at http://lccn.loc.gov/2016007725

CONTENTS

CHAPTER 1: What Are Synthetic Drugs?

Late one night, a Louisville, Kentucky, a mother answered the telephone and learned that her son was in an ambulance headed for Kosair Children's Hospital. He was violently ill and having seizures. Earlier that evening, the teen and his friends had passed around a small bottle with a dropper. Some smoked the liquid inside the bottle using an e-cigarette. Others put a few drops of the liquid on their tongues and then sipped an energy drink. "He never saw the bottle, they had just put it onto his tongue," says the teen's mother. "It happened very quickly. He had an immediate reaction. His heart rate dropped, his oxygen levels dropped—he could have died."[1]

The bottle contained a substance called Cloud Nine, which has been increasingly linked to overdoses, seizures, and aggressive and suicidal behavior. Cloud Nine is a type of synthetic drug known as liquid spice, sometimes known as "Bizarro" or "Mr. Nice Guy." These synthetic drugs often have components that are similar to delta-9-tetrahydrocannabinol (THC), the psychoactive ingredient in marijuana. Yet they are much more dangerous than traditional pot.

According to Martin Redd of the US Drug Enforcement Administration (DEA), the use of liquid synthetic drugs has become a big problem in local middle and high schools. Dr. Amy Hanson, who works in the emergency department at Kosair Children's Hospital agrees; she has seen a spike in high school patients needing emergency treatment after using synthetic drugs. "Kids are starting to experiment with it and it's very, very dangerous," says Redd. "I am quite certain that a majority of parents have either never heard of it, or they probably don't think their kids are doing it."[2]

What Are Synthetic Drugs?

Synthetic drugs are not just one drug—this is a catch-all term for a wide range of chemical products that are constantly changing. Unlike substances such as marijuana or cocaine, synthetics are human-made and do not come from plants. Made in laboratories or in homes, synthetic drugs are designed to mimic naturally occurring illicit drugs. They are sold as easy-to-find and inexpensive alternatives to illegal drugs.

Two of the most popular synthetic drugs are synthetic marijuana and bath salts. Synthetic marijuana comes in the form of dried, shredded plant material, often from the damiana plant, whereas bath salts are typically sold as a white or brown powder and marketed as incense, potpourri, or plant food. They are frequently labeled as "not for human consumption," which makes them not subject to regulation or oversight. This is especially dangerous, considering that they are often much stronger than the traditional drugs they mimic. "Everything about this is a lie," says Barbara Carreno, a spokesperson with the DEA. "They're not potpourri. They're called that as a smoke screen for people naive to drugs."[3]

> "Everything about this is a lie. They're not potpourri. They're called that as a smoke screen for people naive to drugs."[3]
>
> —Barbara Carreno, a spokesperson with the DEA.

Who Is Using Synthetic Drugs?

Since first appearing in the United States around 2008, synthetic drugs have become increasingly popular. The exact number of users is difficult to estimate, but reports from poison control centers and other agencies across the country have shed some light on who is using these drugs. According to the American Association of Poison Control Centers (AAPCC), there were nearly seventeen thousand calls related to synthetic cannabinoids between January 1, 2010, and July 30, 2013. Most of these calls originated in the Midwest and Southeast, and many involved young people. According to the National Institute on Drug Abuse (NIDA), 60 percent of people admitted to an emergency department for

Why People Try Synthetic Marijuana

Although every user is different, a survey of adult patients in a midwestern substance abuse treatment program revealed that most tried synthetic cannabinoids out of curiosity. Other common reasons included the desire to feel good, to relax, or to get high without triggering a positive drug test.

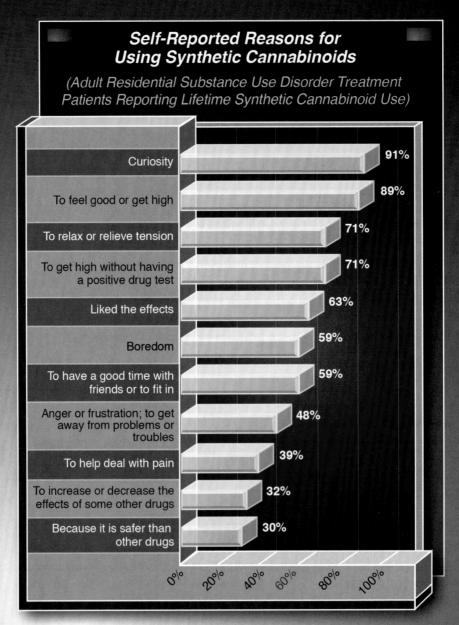

Self-Reported Reasons for Using Synthetic Cannabinoids

(Adult Residential Substance Use Disorder Treatment Patients Reporting Lifetime Synthetic Cannabinoid Use)

Reason	Percentage
Curiosity	91%
To feel good or get high	89%
To relax or relieve tension	71%
To get high without having a positive drug test	71%
Liked the effects	63%
Boredom	59%
To have a good time with friends or to fit in	59%
Anger or frustration; to get away from problems or troubles	48%
To help deal with pain	39%
To increase or decrease the effects of some other drugs	32%
Because it is safer than other drugs	30%

Source: Center for Substance Abuse Research, "Study of Patients in a Midwestern Residential Treatment Program Finds 71% of Those Reporting Synthetic Cannabinoid Use Report Using to Avoid Positive Drug Test," September 8, 2014. www.cesar.umd.edu.

synthetic cannabinoid use are between twelve and twenty years old. Bath salt use is similarly concentrated in the Midwest and Southeast. According to data from the AAPCC, bath salt exposures have been reported in people as young as six to those older than fifty-nine. However, bath salts tend to be most popular with young adults aged twenty to twenty-nine.

According to the NIDA's 2014 Monitoring the Future survey, synthetic marijuana was the third-most popular drug used by high school seniors. This finding is further confirmed by the DEA, which reports that twelve- to seventeen-year-olds are synthetic drugs' biggest user population.

One reason synthetics are so popular with young people is that they are usually inexpensive, and teens buy them with little difficulty from convenience stores, gas stations, and online sites. Synthetic drugs also have a unique chemical structure that is not (yet) easily detected in standard drug tests, which may appeal to some users. According to Garrett, a teen who has smoked spice, "My buddies . . . told me that there was something called synthetic weed that didn't come up on . . . drug tests. My parents were always on me [about that]."[4]

A Toxic Grab Bag of the Unknown

Many people, especially teens and young adults, may think that synthetic drugs are safer than natural drugs, an impression given by the fact that they are legally sold in corner stores and gas stations. However, synthetics are as dangerous and potentially far more damaging than their natural counterparts. They have not undergone safety testing, and it is often unclear what ingredients they contain.

This is because drug makers are constantly tweaking the drugs' chemical formulas to circumvent laws. It is also because different batches of the same drug can contain wildly different chemicals or different concentrations (amounts) of the same chemicals. "There's no consistency to what's in the package," says Mark Ryan, director of the Louisiana Poison Center, whose office tested packets of synthetic drugs to see how much of the active ingredient 3,4-methylenedioxypyrovalerone (MDPV) they contained. "One of them only contained 17 milligrams. One contained 2,000 milligrams."[5] Ryan says that this inconsistency helps explain why some people have a mild reaction to a synthetic drug and others experience severe side effects.

Synthetic drugs are frequently made in underground labs, often in China or other foreign countries. There is no quality control or consistency to the process. Drug makers range from college kids in basements to large operations that mix up huge quantities in industrial mixers. Inconsistent drug making can yield some batches that have low concentrations of the drug and some that have very high concentrations. Thus, two batches made by the same person, even in the same place, can have wildly different concentrations of ingredients. "Is Crazy Monkey today the same as Crazy Monkey tomorrow?" asks Paul Prather, a professor of pharmacology and toxicology at the University of Arkansas for Medical Sciences, about a type of synthetic marijuana. "No way. The makers take some random herb, and spray it with cannabinoid. They're probably using some cheap sprayer to spray it by hand. How *much* synthetic cannabis is in there? You have no idea how much you're getting."[6]

> "Is Crazy Monkey today the same as Crazy Monkey tomorrow? No way. The makers take some random herb, and spray it with cannabinoid. . . . You have no idea how much you're getting."[6]
>
> —Paul Prather, a professor of pharmacology and toxicology at the University of Arkansas for Medical Sciences.

Because of this, it is probably unsurprising that the ingredients printed on a drug's label may be completely inaccurate. "We can analyze one [product] and it will have one drug in it, [and] even from the same store, the same seizure, [the product] right next to it will have a completely different drug,"[7] says Jill Head, a forensic chemist with the DEA's Special Testing and Research Laboratory in Virginia. With a wide range of chemical formulas and potencies, users have no idea what they are taking or the effect it will have on their bodies. One user might smoke spice and experience elevated mood and relaxation, whereas another may smoke the same

Inside a Synthetic Marijuana Operation

Wesley Upchurch, the twenty-four-year-old owner of Pandora Potpourri, works in a cramped garage bay in Columbia, Missouri. He and his one employee can be found huddled over a long, foldout table covered with a pile of plant material, an electronic scale, a stack of Mylar foil packets, and a heat sealer. They mix the plant material with synthetic drug chemicals and let it dry. Then they weigh out portions of the crushed plant material, dump it into a packet, and seal the top. The finished product looks like crushed grass. Each packet is labeled "Bombay Breeze" and is decorated with a meditating cartoon elephant. A disclaimer at the bottom corner cautions in all capital letters that the product is not for consumption. Instead, Upchurch insists that his product is incense and not meant to be smoked.

Despite the warnings, Pandora's synthetic cannabinoids are packed into bongs, smoked, and reviewed on websites for their ability to get users high. Upchurch sells about forty-one thousand packets each month, delivering to fifty stores nationwide and several other wholesalers. He estimates that his company earns about $2.4 million in revenue annually. Retailers who buy his product—like Micah Riggs, who owns a coffee shop in Kansas City, Missouri—say they are not responsible for what people do with the product after they buy it.

drug and end up in a coma. As a result of the unpredictability and variation in ingredients, use can severely damage health, lead to addiction, and even cause death.

Synthetic Cannabinoids

Synthetic cannabinoids, often referred to as synthetic marijuana, are among the most common synthetic drugs in the United States. Cannabinoids are naturally occurring compounds produced by the cannabis plant. One of these cannabinoids, THC, is a mind-altering chemical that produces the psychoactive effects that many marijuana users seek. Synthetic marijuana mimics the effects of THC, but in many cases it is much stronger and can have more side effects than natural marijuana.

Synthetic marijuana is made by spraying chemicals on dried plant material. According to Narconon, the plant most often used is damiana, a flowering herb that is used as an aphrodisiac and mood enhancer. "What happens is the drug . . . is added to a chemical solution and dissolved. The way you would dissolve sugar into ice tea. You make a solution, and it's added to the plant material,"[8] says Head. She says that the mixing and spraying process is often uneven, which creates batches that have varying amounts of the drug. Some batches have little to no chemical on the plant's leaves, whereas others get highly concentrated doses.

Synthetic marijuana is sold in eye-catching packaging under various brand names such as Spice, K2, Blaze, Scooby Doo, Red X Dawn, Paradise, Demon, and Black Magic, names that can appeal to young people. Since 2009 law enforcement has encountered approximately ninety-five different synthetic cannabinoids that are sold as legal alternatives to marijuana. For several years, synthetic cannabinoids were easy to buy in local convenience

Many synthetic drug packages feature bold colors, fanciful characters, and memorable names. These eye-catching packages heighten the appeal for young people.

stores and gas stations. In 2011 the DEA banned five chemicals most frequently found in spice as Schedule I controlled substances, which made it illegal to sell, buy, or possess them. However, manufacturers of synthetic cannabinoids have modified their chemical formulas to create new, legal versions of their products.

Many users smoke synthetic marijuana using a pipe; a water pipe, or bong; or by rolling the drug-laced plant material in cigarette papers. Alternatively, some synthetic cannabinoids come in liquid form so that they can be vaporized using electronic cigarettes or drunk as part of an herbal infusion. Users report that the drugs produce effects similar to marijuana, such as elevated mood, relaxation, and altered perception. The high from this drug begins immediately after the substance enters the brain and typically lasts for about one to three hours. In some cases the effects of synthetic marijuana are much stronger than natural marijuana, with users reporting extreme anxiety, paranoia, and hallucinations.

Synthetic Cathinones (Bath Salts)

Synthetic cathinones are a family of drugs that contain one or more human-made chemicals that are related to cathinone, an amphetamine-like drug found naturally in the khat plant. These chemicals include mephedrone, methylone, and MDPV. These psychoactive drugs mimic the effects of amphetamines and hallucinogens such as MDMA, methamphetamine, and cocaine.

Known as bath salts and sold on the street under names such as Boom and Cosmic Blast, synthetic cathinones typically come in a white or brown crystalline powder. Manufacturers package the powder in small plastic or foil packages. These are often marketed as bath salts, research chemicals, jewelry cleaner, or plant food. Sometimes these substances are put into gelatin capsules. Drug makers label these packages "not for human consumption" to obscure the fact that these products are used as a psychoactive drug. Typically, synthetic cathinone products are sold at smoke shops, convenience stores, and gas stations, as well as over the Internet. According to the DEA, many are manufactured in eastern Asia and distributed throughout Europe, North America, Australia, and other areas of the world.

Synthetic cathinones such as bath salts are typically snorted or snuffed up the nose. They can also be taken orally, smoked, or dissolved in a solution and then injected into a user's vein. Synthetic cathinones can make users feel euphoric, as well as increase their sociability and sex drive. Some users, however, feel paranoid, become agitated, and even hallucinate. In some cases use of these drugs can lead to psychotic, violent behavior and even death. In 2012, for example, thirty-one-year-old Jesse Claflin from Syracuse, New York, held a knife to the throat of a five-year-old boy while high on bath salts. In another example, thirty-one-year-old Travis Bonham fatally shot his mother and girlfriend in 2015 at his central Ohio home while high on bath salts.

Synthetic Hallucinogens

A third category of synthetic drugs, synthetic hallucinogens, mimic the effects of hallucinogenic drugs such as LSD (aka, acid), but at a lower price. "Dealers see a tremendous opportunity to sell this particular drug for a lot cheaper,"[9] says Dr. Joji Suzuki, director of the Division of Addiction Psychiatry at Brigham and Women's Hospital in Boston. These drugs are sold and taken as tablets or capsules. In some cases they come in liquid form and are dropped onto blotting paper, sugar cubes, or gelatin sheets and ingested.

> "My son was not a reckless person. . . . He would never have tried something he knew was that dangerous."[10]
>
> —Susan Wadsworth, whose son Noah died after taking synthetic drugs.

Synthetic hallucinogens are among the most powerful and potentially deadly synthetic drugs sold around the country. N-bomb, a synthetic hallucinogen that mimics illegal LSD, has been connected to numerous deaths and hospitalizations. In January 2013, for example, eighteen-year-old Noah Carrasco lost consciousness after taking a dose of N-bomb via nose drops. At first friends thought he just needed to sleep it off. When he continued to be unresponsive, they became concerned and drove him to the hospital. "He'd been dead already at least for a couple of hours," says Susan Wadsworth, Carrasco's mother. "They didn't know that that's what they were taking. My

Although most buyers and sellers know the purpose of bath salts (pictured), they are typically labeled "not for human consumption." In reality, bath salts are used as a psychoactive drug.

son was not a reckless person. He decided to try what he thought was acid, and obviously I didn't know this at the time. But he would never have tried something he knew was that dangerous."[10]

Changing Formulas to Keep Ahead of the Law

Since 2011 all fifty states have placed some sort of ban on synthetic drugs. In July 2012 the US government passed the Synthetic Drug Abuse Prevention Act, which places a number of synthetic substances in the most restrictive category of controlled substances. Fifteen synthetic cannabinoid compounds, two synthetic cathinone compounds, and nine synthetic hallucinogens are restricted under this law. In addition, an additional ten synthetic cathinones were placed under a temporary ban by the DEA in 2014.

However, drug makers have responded by creating new substances that are chemically similar to banned substances, yet different enough that they are technically not prohibited by law.

Flakka: A Second-Generation Bath Salt

One of the newest synthetic drugs to emerge is flakka, which is made from a compound called alpha-PVP, a chemical related to cathinone. Alpha-PVP is a stimulant, which produces feelings of euphoria and increases alertness and motor activity. Called "gravel" in some areas of the United States because of its white crystal chunks that look like aquarium gravel, flakka produces a high similar to that of cocaine. A single dose of flakka is cheap and sells for as little as three to five dollars. Dealers often target young or poor people to buy the drug.

Because flakka is so potent, users only need a small amount to feel its effects. Just a tiny bit more of the drug can cause severe and unintended effects, giving it the potential to be much more dangerous than other potent drugs like cocaine. "It's so difficult to control the exact dose [of flakka]," says Jim Hall, an epidemiologist at Nova Southeastern University in Fort Lauderdale, Florida. "Just a little bit of difference in how much is consumed can be the difference between getting high and dying. It's that critical."

Quoted in Carina Storrs, "What Is Flakka (aka Gravel) and Why Is It More Dangerous than Cocaine?," CNN, May 26, 2015. www.cnn.com.

Keeping up with these changes is very difficult, because it can take years to get a new chemical or drug permanently added to the federal list of controlled substances and deemed illegal. As states and the federal government race to ban these chemical compounds, drug makers stay one step ahead of legislation by constantly changing their chemical formulas. "The chemical companies are altering the compound ever so slightly to avoid our laws," explains John Scherbenske, who oversees the DEA's Synthetic Drugs and Chemicals Section. "Once they alter that chemical, it is no longer a controlled substance."[11]

This cat-and-mouse game drives the evolution and development of synthetic drugs. For example, in the case of N-bomb, the federal government has banned the active chemical in one version of the drug—2C-I; however, chemists have simply created new variations of the drug to avoid the ban. Similarly, "flakka largely emerged as a replacement to MDPV [in bath salts],"[12] explains Lucas Watterson of Temple University's School of Medicine Center for Substance Abuse Research. In March 2014 the DEA put a temporary ban on flakka, but manufacturers got around that by labeling the product "not for human consumption." A federal ban on flakka may come within several years, but Watterson says that this effort will involve the same problem that exists in banning all synthetic drugs—that even when one type is banned, another type quickly emerges to take its place.

According to the DEA, it takes a chemist only a few weeks to change a molecule and put a new synthetic drug on the streets. Indeed, the DEA estimates that five new synthetic drug compounds are introduced in the United States every month. As Watterson puts it, "It's sort of a flavor of the month."[13] Sergeant Mark Clark, a Scottsdale, Arizona, police spokesperson, agrees: "What you have is some amateur chemists who are trying to change the formulation of a drug that's been declared an illegal substance to try to stay ahead of the law." He says it is critical that people know that even slight variations in the synthetic drugs can have far-ranging effects. "Kids—and it's mostly kids who are taking this—need to understand that this chemical variant could be changed by a very, very little bit and it can prove to be very harmful."[14]

> "The chemical companies are altering the compound ever so slightly to avoid our laws. Once they alter that chemical, it is no longer a controlled substance."[11]
>
> —John Scherbenske of the DEA's Synthetic Drugs and Chemicals Section.

Unknown and Unpredictable

Synthetic drugs have emerged as some of the most dangerous drugs available. These compounds are often significantly stronger than the illicit drugs that they are meant to replace. And although many people believe that synthetic drugs are a safe way to get high, synthetics are anything but safe. DEA agent Bruce Goldberg does not mince words when he talks about the risks of taking synthetic substances that contain unknown and unpredictable ingredients. He says, "Kids are playing Russian roulette with their lives."[15]

CHAPTER 2: Effects of Synthetic Drug Use

In June 2012 Elijah Stai and his foster brother Justin Rippentrop traveled to Grand Forks, North Dakota, to celebrate Stai's eighteenth birthday. While visiting Stai's cousin, they were offered a bag of chocolates laced with a white powder. The cousin's boyfriend told them that the powder was an extract from psychedelic mushrooms. The two young men ate the bag of drug-laced chocolates and shortly after began to experience hallucinations. "The trees looked like cauliflowers like dancing around," says Rippentrop. "The sidewalks were swooping up and down like a roller coaster, and the grass was shooting up to the sky."[16]

Rippentrop, who had used psychedelic mushrooms before, says that he quickly noticed that something was different this time. Then Stai began to convulse uncontrollably. He foamed at the mouth and hit his head. An ambulance rushed Stai to the hospital, where doctors determined that he had experienced multiple organ failure and had also gone into cardiac arrest. A few hours after taking the drug, Stai was ruled brain dead and was kept alive by life support machines. Three days later, Stai's family made the difficult decision to disconnect his life support. He died shortly after the machines were turned off.

A week after Stai's death, the lab identified that the powder in the chocolate Stai had eaten was not from psychedelic mushrooms. Instead, it was a synthetic designer drug—a form of N-bomb, a synthetic that imitates LSD. This synthetic drug was so potent that an amount the size of a few grains of salt is enough to produce a high.

Strong and Unpredictable

Synthetic drugs mimic the effects of plant-based drugs. Synthetic-cannabinoid users report effects similar to those produced by marijuana, such as elevated mood, relaxation, altered perceptions, and a detachment from reality. Synthetics such as bath salts mimic the effects of cocaine or methamphetamine. Stimulant effects such as rapid heartbeat, increased blood pressure, and disrupted sleep may occur shortly after use. Mentally, users may experience euphoria, alertness, and agitation. A user will probably not feel hungry, and may feel dizzy, experience a rise in body temperature, and have tense muscles. The effects of these drugs last about three to four hours.

Yet in many cases synthetic drugs can be stronger and more unpredictable than the drugs they imitate. The effects a user experiences depends on the type of drug and even the particular batch. After using synthetic marijuana, some people have experienced severe psychotic behavior. They report intense paranoia, extreme anxiety, hallucinations, aggression, and suicidal thoughts. Others have landed in the emergency room for rapid heart rate, vomiting, and violent behavior. Synthetic cannabinoids can raise a user's blood pressure to dangerous levels, reduce blood supply to the heart, and cause kidney damage and seizures.

> **"The trees looked like cauliflowers like dancing around. The sidewalks were swooping up and down like a roller coaster, and the grass was shooting up to the sky."[16]**
>
> —Justin Rippentrop, a synthetic drug user whose foster brother died after ingesting a synthetic designer drug.

Synthetic bath salts can also have stronger and more unpredictable effects than intended, including hallucinations and psychotic delusions. Users may also experience increased paranoia and aggression, which can lead to violent behavior, assault, murder, and suicide. Physically, synthetic bath salts can damage the liver and kidneys, increase blood pressure, and cause a heart attack or stroke. For some people, high doses of these drugs can trigger intense and extended panic attacks.

Effects on the Brain

Synthetic drugs may more strongly affect users because of how they affect the brain. The human brain has natural cannabinoid

Natural and Synthetic Marijuana Are Not the Same

Although synthetic cannabinoids are intended to mimic natural marijuana, they have more serious and potentially life-threatening effects on the body and brain. The constantly changing formulas and ingredients in synthetic cannabinoids add to the potential for unexpected and serious physical effects.

Marijuana	Synthetic Cannabinoids
Effects on the Brain	**Effects on the Brain**
Paranoia	Paranoid delusions
Anxiety	Anxiety
Depression	Depression
Slow reaction time	Suicidal thoughts
Distorted sense of time	Psychosis
Short-term memory loss	Severe agitation
Feeling of relaxation	Inability to feel pain
Strange feelings of "random" thinking	Hallucinations
	Total memory loss

Marijuana	Synthetic Cannabinoids
Physical effects	**Physical effects**
Elevated blood pressure	Extremely high blood pressure (stroke range)
Red eyes	Dilated pupils, red eyes
Dry mouth	Glazed expression
Increased breathing rate	Inability to speak
Faster heart rate	Rapid heart rate (possible heart attack)
Increased appetite	Nausea and vomiting
Relaxed muscles	Kidney failure
	Tremors
	Muscle cramps, seizures, and temporary paralysis

Source: Abigail Hauslohner and Peter Hermann, "The Scariest Thing About Synthetic Drugs Is Everything That's Unknown," *Washington Post*, July 18, 2015. www.washingtonpost.com.

chemicals that work as neurotransmitters, sending chemical messages between neurons and nerve cells throughout the body's central nervous system. Messages are sent to areas of the brain that control pleasure, memory, thinking, concentration, movement and coordination, the senses, and time perception. The main psychoactive ingredient in natural marijuana, THC, is similar to the human body's natural chemicals. It attaches to cannabinoid receptors in the brain, activating neurons and disrupting several mental and physical functions. This is what causes users to feel high.

Researchers have found that compounds in synthetic cannabinoids bind more strongly to the brain's receptors than those in natural marijuana, however. Synthetics activate the receptors with maximum efficacy—that is, the maximum effect a drug can produce—and to a greater extent than natural THC. "Synthetic cannabinoids are tailor-made to hit cannabinoid receptors—and hit [them] hard," says Jeff Lapoint, an emergency room doctor and medical toxicologist. "This is *not* marijuana. Its action in the brain may be similar but the physical effect is so different."[17]

In addition, synthetics are highly potent, meaning it takes much less of the drug to produce a high. "Its potency can be up to one hundred or more times greater than THC," says Paul Prather, a professor of pharmacology and toxicology at the University of Arkansas for Medical Sciences. In Prather's opinion, being more effective and more potent explains why "their use may result in [the] development of life-threatening adverse effects."[18]

> **"Synthetic cannabinoids are tailor-made to hit cannabinoid receptors—and hit [them] hard. This is *not* marijuana."[17]**
>
> —Jeff Lapoint, an emergency room doctor and medical toxicologist.

Cannabinoid receptors are located on neurons throughout the brain, which means that synthetic marijuana can affect many different brain functions and thus affect the cardiac, respiratory, and gastrointestinal systems. According to Yasmin Hurd, a professor of psychiatry, pharmacology, and neuroscience at Mount Sinai Medical Center, the distribution of cannabinoid receptors throughout the brain plays a role in making synthetics so dangerous. Of the receptors, she says, "Where they're located is important—their presence in the hippocampus would [explain] their memory effects; their presence in seizure initiation areas in the temporal cortex is why they lead to seizures. And in the prefrontal cortex, this is probably why you see stronger psychosis with synthetic cannabinoids."[19]

Long Lasting and Difficult to Treat

Typically, the effects of natural marijuana or cocaine wear off as a user's body metabolizes the drug. Cocaine, methamphetamine, or marijuana enter the user's bloodstream and begin to wear off within a few hours. For synthetics like bath salts, however, the effects last much longer and are more difficult to treat. "Some patients were in the hospital for 5 days, 10 days, 14 days," says Mark Ryan, director of the Louisiana Poison Center, who has studied the rise of synthetic drug–related emergency events. "In some cases, they were under heavy sedation. As you try to taper off the sedation, the paranoia came back [as did] the delusions."[20]

Researchers suspect that the particular way synthetics work in the brain may explain why their effects last so long. Typically, the human body deactivates a drug as it metabolizes it. But according to Prather, some of the substances that form when synthetic cannabis is metabolized also bind to the brain's receptors, which does not happen with the THC in natural marijuana. Prather says that this may be why the body is less able to deactivate synthetics. In addition, Prather points out that synthetic cannabis does not contain cannabidiol, a substance that is present in natural marijuana. Cannabidiol appears to soften some of the adverse effects of THC. The lack of cannabidiol may explain why synthetic cannabinoids are often more powerful and toxic than natural marijuana.

The way synthetic drugs affect dopamine may also explain their power and longevity. Dopamine is a neurotransmitter that is involved in the brain's reward centers and feelings of pleasure. In the brain, dopamine moves from one neuron to another, sending a signal. Once sent, dopamine retreats back into the neuron in a process called reuptake. The release and reuptake of dopamine causes feelings of pleasure, exhilaration, and well-being. Dopamine also affects memory, learning, motivation, and motor control.

Paying the Ultimate Price

Synthetic drugs have killed users. One was eighteen-year-old Christian Bjerk, who in 2012 was found dead on the sidewalk near his Grand Forks, North Dakota, home. The previous night Bjerk had gone out to buy gas. He ran into some friends and decided to go to a house party, where they all did a synthetic drug known as N-bomb. Near Bjerk's body, police found the two other teens, one naked on a bench and the other screaming at a parked car.

Since their son's death, Bjerk's parents have become activists, educating others about the dangers of synthetic drugs and lobbying for legislation to ban synthetics. "Christian was—he was a child, he was our flesh and blood, he was someone who was so important to us that we would've given our lives for him," says his father, Keith Bjerk. "It is now our job to get the word out there to the rest of the people so that no other families have to go through this kind of thing and to honor our son."

Quoted in Drew Griffin and Nelli Black, "Deadly High: How Synthetic Drugs Are Killing Kids," CNN, December 2, 2014. www.cnn.com.

Drugs like methamphetamine, amphetamines, and cocaine produce a high by causing excess dopamine in the brain, although they do so in different ways. Methamphetamine and amphetamines cause excess dopamine to surge between the neurons, overstimulating them and the brain's reward centers. In contrast, cocaine is a reuptake inhibitor. It blocks the reuptake of the dopamine back into the cell, leaving excess dopamine in the spaces between the brain's neurons. This overstimulates the neurons and generates a rush of energy and a euphoric high.

Researchers have found that synthetic drugs like bath salts also increase dopamine levels. Louis De Felice, a neuroscientist at VCU School of Medicine, worked with a team of researchers to test the chemicals present in bath salts. They found that bath salts contain mephedrone, which acts like an amphetamine and causes neurons to release excessive amounts of dopamine. Another bath salt chemical, MDPV, produced a different effect. It worked like cocaine, blocking the reuptake of dopamine back into the neurons. De Felice's team concluded that taking bath salts was therefore like using amphetamines and cocaine at the same time. One chemical causes the brain's neurons to release excess amounts of dopamine, which are then blocked from reentering the cell by another chemical.

De Felice described the phenomenon as being like using a kitchen sink, with the space between the brain's neurons as the sink and the water as dopamine. Neurons release dopamine through the faucet into the sink. The sink's drain allows some of the water to flow back into the cell. But bath salts turn the faucet on high and also close the drain. Eventually, the dopamine floods the brain. "In all the areas where dopamine is important, you've got too much of it," says De Felice. "When you realize the implications of that for drugs people take, you're like, oh my gosh, what an insidious combination this is."[21]

Organ Damage

Synthetic drugs also affect the body. Their active ingredients can damage internal organs, including the heart, lungs, and kidneys. Abnormal heart rhythms and heart attacks have been associated with ingesting synthetic marijuana.

People who use synthetic marijuana may be at risk of developing blood clots and strokes. In 2013 researchers from the University of South Florida published case studies of two healthy siblings, aged twenty-six and nineteen, who experienced acute ischemic strokes soon after smoking spice. An ischemic stroke happens when an artery in the brain is blocked by a blood clot. Doctors found that both siblings had a stroke caused by a blood clot in the brain. The siblings were otherwise healthy, and doctors found that neither one had a genetic condition that made him or her more likely to have a stroke.

John C.M. Brust, a member of the Neurological Institute of New York, agrees that synthetic marijuana may cause strokes. He points out that there have been several cases in which natural marijuana has caused strokes. He reasons that since synthetic versions of marijuana are even more potent, synthetics likely have the ability to cause strokes, too. "If marijuana can cause ischemic

Synthetic Marijuana Spikes Calls to Poison Centers

In 2015, poison control centers across the United States reported a 229 percent increase in synthetic marijuana–related calls from January to May compared to the same period in 2014. Calls were particularly heavy between March and May. Callers reported symptoms such as rapid heart rate, drowsiness, and vomiting. Fifteen of these calls resulted in death.

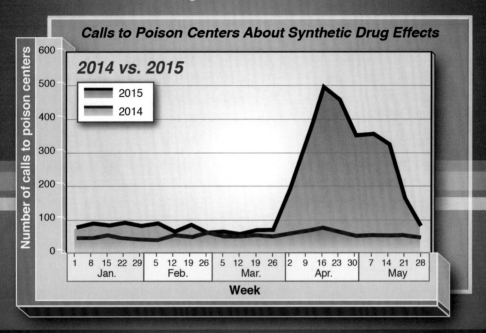

Calls to Poison Centers About Synthetic Drug Effects

2014 vs. 2015

Legend:
- 2015
- 2014

Y-axis: Number of calls to poison centers (0, 100, 200, 300, 400, 500, 600)

X-axis: Week
- Jan.: 1, 8, 15, 22, 29
- Feb.: 5, 12, 19, 26
- Mar.: 5, 12, 19, 26
- Apr.: 2, 9, 16, 23, 30
- May: 7, 14, 21, 28

Source: Catherine Woods, "Synthetic Marijuana Triggers Spike in Suspected Poisonings," *PBS Newshour*, June 11, 2015. www.pbs.org.

stroke, and if anything pot can do spice can do better, neurologists will likely encounter increasing numbers of spice-associated strokes in the years ahead,"[22] he warns.

Synthetic drugs can also cause extensive lung damage. In 2011 Brandon Rice, an eighth grader from Pennsylvania, smoked synthetic marijuana out of a PEZ candy dispenser. The chemicals in the drugs burned and damaged his lungs to the point that he was put on a respirator in June 2011. He underwent a double lung transplant a few months later, in September 2011. In December of that same year, however, Brandon died from complications related to the transplant.

Synthetic drugs and the toxic chemicals that they contain have also been linked to kidney damage. In 2013 researchers at the University of Alabama–Birmingham reported that smoking synthetic marijuana caused acute kidney injury (AKI). They detailed the cases of four previously healthy young men who developed AKI after ingesting synthetic marijuana. Each patient experienced nausea, vomiting, and abdominal pain over a nine-week period. Three excreted an abnormally small volume of urine, and the fourth had reduced blood flow to the kidney. Three patients showed acute tubular necrosis, a condition that if left untreated can cause the kidneys to shut down. Eventually, all four patients recovered their kidney function without needing dialysis. The researchers suspect that an additive in the synthetic marijuana, not the cannabinoid itself, was responsible for the damage.

Violent Behavior

Synthetics do not just affect the body; across the United States they have been linked to episodes of bizarre, violent, and potentially deadly behavior. Clint Thurgood, a licensed clinical social worker with McKay-Dee Hospital in Ogden, Utah, has seen many teens come to the emergency room with psychotic symptoms after using spice or bath salts. "I have personally met with teens who have attempted suicide, became assaultive, or otherwise put others' lives at risk because of their drug-induced psychosis,"[23] he says. In the midst of a violent episode, users can become dangerous to themselves and everyone around them.

"They strip off their clothes and run outdoors, acting very violent with adrenaline-surged strength. It can take four or more cops to hold them down."[24]

—Jim Hall, epidemiologist.

Flakka has been particularly linked to violent behavior. It can trigger fits of screaming rage and vivid hallucinations. Users may also take off their clothes in sweaty, delusional fits because the drug can cause body temperatures to rise as high as 106°F (41°C). "They strip off their clothes and run outdoors, acting very violent with adrenaline-surged strength," says epidemiologist Jim Hall. "It can take four or more cops to hold them down."[24] In April 2015, for example, Fort Lauderdale police arrested a man high on flakka

Synthetics in War

Soldiers in Syria are turning to synthetic drugs to help them fight the years-long civil war that has ravaged that country. Their drug of choice is Captagon, a highly addictive synthetic drug produced in Syria and available across the Middle East. The drug is easy to produce and sells for less than twenty dollars a tablet. Based on the original synthetic drug fenethylline, it acts as a powerful amphetamine. After taking Captagon, soldiers quickly experience a euphoric intensity that allows them to stay up for days and kill with a reckless abandon. Users say it makes them feel powerful and fearless. One Syrian who fought as a soldier describes how the drug gives soldiers incredible energy and courage:

> If there were 10 people in front of you, you could catch them and kill them. You're awake all the time. You don't have any problems, you don't even think about sleeping, you don't think to leave the checkpoint. It gives you great courage and power. If the leader told you to go break into a military barracks, I will break in with a brave heart and without any feeling of fear at all—you're not even tired.

Quoted in Peter Holley, "The Tiny Pill Fueling Syria's War and Turning Fighters into Superhuman Soldiers," *Washington Post*, November 19, 2015. www.washingtonpost.com.

after he ran down a major roadway naked. The man told officers that people were chasing him; he said they had stolen his clothes and he wanted to get hit by a car so they would stop chasing him. Another example comes from Syracuse, New York, where in 2015 police officers responded to several calls about people high on synthetic drugs who are foaming at the mouth and trying to box with cars.

Medical Emergencies

For all of these reasons, synthetic drugs have been linked to an increase in emergency room visits, calls to poison control centers, and hospitalizations across the country. According to a June 2015 report by the Centers for Disease Control and Prevention, synthetic marijuana–related emergency calls to poison control centers increased 229 percent between January and May 2015, compared to the same period in 2014. People reported symptoms such as agitation, increased heart rate, drowsiness, and vomiting. More than 11 percent of the calls dealt with potentially life-threatening, disabling, or disfiguring reactions to the drug. In some people synthetic drug use has led to a brain hemorrhage, or bleeding around the brain. The resulting brain damage can cause significant disruption of many brain-controlled functions, including movement and speech. Even with extensive rehabilitation, some patients may be left with long-term weakness, experience memory or sensory problems, and suffer from seizures. In some cases, a brain hemorrhage can be fatal.

Dr. Chris Hoyte, an assistant professor of emergency medicine and medical toxicology, is not surprised by this news. He says that contaminated or poorly created synthetic drugs can and do cause medical emergencies. He has seen patients go into renal failure, have heart attacks, or experience seizures after using synthetics. "You don't know what you're getting," says Hoyte.

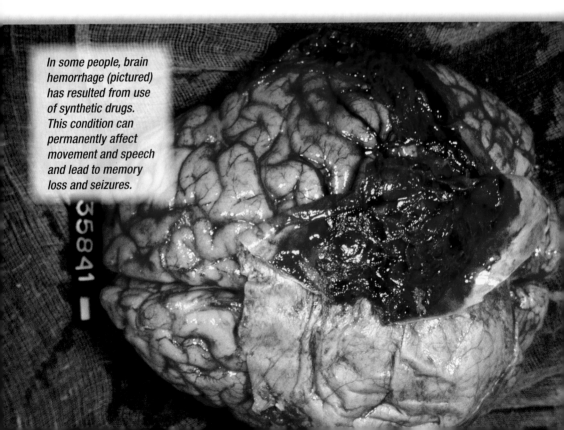

In some people, brain hemorrhage (pictured) has resulted from use of synthetic drugs. This condition can permanently affect movement and speech and lead to memory loss and seizures.

"People they come in agitated [or] really, really sleepy, where they have to be intubated or put on a mechanical ventilator."[25]

According to the AAPCC, in the first three weeks of April 2015, state poison control centers nationwide received about one thousand reports of bad reactions to synthetic marijuana, more than twice the total from January through March 2015. Health departments in several states—including Alabama, Mississippi, and New York—issued alerts about spice users being rushed to hospitals for extreme anxiety, violent behavior, delusions, and in some cases, death. Two cases involved Jeffrey and Joey Stallings, twenty-four- and twenty-nine-year-old brothers from McComb, Mississippi. After the brothers smoked a form of synthetic marijuana, Jeffrey became delusional and extremely violent, and Joey became extremely agitated. Their mother rushed both young men to the hospital, where they were admitted for about a week; both may have permanent kidney damage.

Louisiana is another place where hospitals reported an increase in synthetics-related visits in 2015. "We had one hospital in the Baton Rouge area that saw over 110 cases in February. That's a huge spike,"[26] says Mark Ryan. Northern Utah has also reported an increase in patients who have taken synthetic drugs. "Our physicians are seeing an increase in . . . spice in particular,"[27] says Janet Smith, director of emergency services at Ogden Regional Medical Center. Smith reports that people who have taken bath salts are treated for agitation, increased heart rate, high blood pressure, fever, hallucinations, paranoia, suicidal thoughts, and delusions, whereas synthetic marijuana users are treated for seizures, vomiting, numbness and tingling, high blood pressure, headache, increased heart rate, an inability to speak, and anxiety and panic attacks. The drugs even put some users into a coma.

Tragic Consequences

In some cases, using a synthetic drug just once can have tragic and long-lasting consequences. In December 2012 sixteen-year-old Emily Bauer smoked synthetic marijuana, which she bought from a local gas station. After smoking it, Bauer thought she had a migraine and decided to lie down. When she woke up, she stumbled and was slurring her words. She entered a psychotic state, experiencing hallucinations and violent outbursts. Her family called for an ambulance to take her to the hospital, where she was admitted to the intensive care unit (ICU). There, she bit the guardrails and attempted to bite those who helped her. "We thought once she comes down off the drug, we'd take her home," said Bauer's older sister. "We didn't think it was as big of a deal until 24 hours later she was still violent and hurting herself. We realized you're not supposed to stay high this long."[28]

To protect her body, doctors put Bauer into an induced coma. Tests showed that every one of her major organs was damaged. "Her heart, lungs, kidney, liver," says Tonya Bauer, Emily's mother. "She had a fever. They had given her antibiotics and tried all different kinds of medicines, everything."[29]

After Bauer had been in the coma a few days, doctors performed a magnetic resonance imaging scan on her brain and saw she had suffered several severe strokes. The strokes were caused by severe vasculitis, a condition in which contracting blood vessels constrict the flow of blood and cut off oxygen to the brain. Brain scans showed that nearly 70 percent of her brain was damaged. Doctors told her family that if she survived, she would be severely disabled and unable to recognize them, eat on her own, or use her arms or legs.

Over the next three years, Bauer's condition improved, although she still has significant impairment. After numerous sessions of physical and occupational therapy, she has regained some of her vision and has some use of her hands. Yet Bauer remains in a wheelchair and depends on her family for everyday needs. "I can still see stuff, but not really," Bauer says. "Sometimes my brain doesn't understand what it's seeing. I can't read or write. I have to have a person with me all day."[30] Her family feeds, bathes, and dresses her and helps her go to the bathroom. "She lost all of her freedom and independence and privacy," says her mother. "No drug is worth that."[31]

> "She lost all of her freedom and independence and privacy. No drug is worth that."[31]
>
> —Tonya Bauer, whose daughter is severely disabled after using synthetic drugs.

As Bauer's case illustrates, the effects of synthetic drug use can be devastating. Although many people assume that they are safe, these drugs can cause long-lasting and permanent damage. "Whether it's the users who consume them, the families that suffer the aftermath, or the law enforcement officers who must deal with both, synthetic drugs are destroying many lives," says Ohio attorney general Mike DeWine. "People mistakenly think that, because this stuff comes in what appear to be commercial packages and is readily available over the counter and on the Internet, it's safe. It's not."[32]

CHAPTER 3: How Addictive Are Synthetic Drugs?

In high school Dylan Evans was an honor student with a good work ethic and an appreciation for education, values instilled in him by his mother, a high school teacher. Evans pushed himself to study hard; he scored high on the ACT exam and worked over the summers to save money for college. He graduated from high school with a 3.97 grade point average and was named salutatorian of his senior class. His efforts also earned him an academic scholarship to Middle Tennessee State University in Murfreesboro, Tennessee.

During his first semester of college, Evans experimented with synthetic drugs. He bought a package of Molly's Plant Food that was commonly sold at convenience stores and tobacco shops. Evans thought it was safe because it was legal. Yet within a few months, Evans became addicted. He spent all the money he had saved on the drug. When he ran out, he stole valuables from his mother and sold them to buy drugs. He also charged thousands of dollars on his mother's credit card. "I lied to myself. I told myself I could control it,"[33] he says.

Within nine months, Evans had dropped out of school and lost his scholarship. He also almost lost his life after overdosing and attempting suicide in the hospital. Eventually, Evans decided to get help and entered rehab for his addiction to synthetic drugs. Now he talks to kids about what can happen to users. "This stuff is dangerous," he says. "It took just about everything I had from me." He says it helps him feel better to help others avoid the mistakes he made. "It's a day to day thing," says Evans. "Today I don't have to use drugs because I talked to these kids."[34]

Regular Use Leads to Addiction

As Evans experienced, regularly using synthetic drugs can make some people addicted to them. According to the NIDA, addiction is a chronic, relapsing brain disease characterized by compulsive drug seeking and use, regardless of harm or consequences. Addictive drugs change the brain's structure and how it works. These changes can be long lasting and drive harmful behavior.

Although research into their addictive potential is still young, early indications suggest that synthetic drugs—particularly synthetic cathinones (bath salts)—have the potential to be highly abused and very addictive. In a 2013 study, researchers from the Scripps Research Institute (TSRI) found that MDPV, an active ingredient in bath salts, is more addictive than methamphetamine, one of the most addictive illegal drugs. In the study, researchers allowed rats to self-administer either MDPV or methamphetamine by pressing a lever that delivered the drug intravenously. Like humans, rats can become easily addicted, making them good models for studying the effects of drugs.

Researchers tested how much drug the rats craved by increasing the number of lever pushes needed to get a dose. "We observed that rats emitted about 60 presses on average for a dose of methamphetamine but up to about 600 for MDPV—some rats would even emit 3,000 lever presses for a single hit of MDPV," says study author Shawn M. Aarde. "If you consider these lever presses a measure of how much a rat will work to get a drug infusion, then these rats worked more than 10 times harder to get MDPV."[35]

The researchers also observed the rats engaging in repetitive behaviors that did not seem to have any clear goal. For example, some MDPV-addicted rats repeatedly licked the clear plastic walls of the chamber, a behavior that continued nonstop. This is similar to how humans high on MDPV have been observed engaging in meaningless repetitive motions and behaviors. For example, some people who are addicted to bath salts or methamphetamine grind their teeth, pick their skin, or exhibit other repetitive behaviors.

Research has shown that the active ingredient in bath salts is even more addictive than methamphetamine (pictured here in crystal form). This is a concern because meth is considered to be one of the most addictive illegal drugs.

Flakka may be just as potent and addictive. In 2015 researchers at TSRI compared rats' response to alpha-PVP, the main ingredient in flakka, and MDPV. Similar to the previous study, the rats were trained to press a lever to administer an intravenous dose. As researchers increased the number of lever presses needed to get a dose, the rats continued to press, up to hundreds of times, to get the drug. In the study, the rats were just as likely to press the lever for alpha-PVP as they were for MDPV, suggesting that alpha-PVP is just as addictive as MDPV. "Animals will self-administer MDPV like no drug I have ever seen," says Tobin J. Dickerson, co-senior author of the study. "Our data show that flakka is as potent as MDPV, making it a very good stimulant, arguably with worse addiction liability than methamphetamine."[36]

Signs of Synthetic Drug Addiction

Synthetic drug addiction has several warning signs, the most obvious of which is the inability to stop using the drug. Once addicted, people compulsively crave the drug and cannot stop using it, even if it interferes with other aspects of their lives. Shyanne from Bakersfield, California, discovered that her twenty-two-year-old son was using spice in 2012. Now, she says, he is addicted. She explains, "He's gotten to the point where he's homeless, because the drug is more important to him than his family." Shyanne says the physical aspects of her son's addiction are horrible to witness. "He throws up blood, he turns grey and almost passes out," she says. "He doesn't care if he lives or dies. It's just, when is he going to get this next bag of spice."[37]

Daniel Blankenberg, a twenty-year-old former spice addict, says he did not care about anything when he was addicted to that drug. Smoking it made him feel crazy, but he felt worse if he did not smoke. "I didn't care about myself. I'd go without eating, I'd go without changing clothes without showering I just didn't care. I didn't have no respect for myself not anybody else," says Blankenberg. One time, he was arrested for spice possession. Another time, he almost died. "I just passed out driving," he says. "Flipped the car six times and woke up ten days later in ICU [from] a coma."[38]

> "He throws up blood, he turns grey and almost passes out. He doesn't care if he lives or dies. It's just, when is he going to get this next bag of spice."[37]
>
> —Shyanne, whose son is addicted to synthetic drugs.

Those who are addicted often choose drug use over activities that used to give them pleasure. Instead of going to a family gathering, they might stay home to get high. They might spend all their money on their habit and have nothing left over to go out to dinner with friends. This is what twenty-one-year-old Hanna did during the time she was addicted to bath salts. "I pretty much stopped doing everything. I stopped going to my ballet class; I stopped going to work," she says. "I thought I was being followed everywhere, so I just stopped wanting to go places."[39]

To test the extent to which synthetic drugs replace a person's hobbies or other pleasurable endeavors, TSRI researchers also examined how MDPV affected rats' wheel running, a normally pleasurable activity for them. They found that as the rats self-administered more MDPV, they ran on the wheel significantly less, indicating that this normally pleasurable activity was less appealing to them than

New York City police come to the aid of a man who is acting strange after using the synthetic marijuana known as spice. Synthetic drug use—and addiction—can lead to bizarre and dangerous behavior.

MDPV. The researchers also found that some of the rats did not increase their use of MDPV gradually, but instead went from occasional use to bingeing on as much as they could get. "That was when they stopped using the wheel—that very day they binged," says Michael A. Taffe, an associate professor at TSRI and one of the study coauthors. "In subsequent sessions, the bingers' intake would stay high and they wouldn't run much on the wheel. We think it's a good model of the ways in which—and the speed with which—drugs can supplant other rewarding things we normally do."[40]

Tolerance and Dependence

Over time, regularly using synthetic drugs can lead a person to build up a tolerance. According to the NIDA, tolerance occurs when a user no longer responds to a drug in the way that he or she first did. Tolerance builds when a person needs to take a higher dose of a drug to experience the same effects.

In addition to raising tolerance, repeated use of synthetic drugs also causes dependence. Dependence occurs when a user's brain adapts to the presence of a drug and only functions normally when the drug is present. Once dependence forms, a user will experience withdrawal symptoms when the drug is removed. These symptoms can range from mild to life threatening. Withdrawal from synthetic marijuana includes uncontrollable vomiting, nausea, loss of appetite, extreme sweating, insomnia, and depression. Withdrawal from synthetic cathinones may cause depression, anxiety, tremors, difficulty sleeping, and paranoia. Users will thus get high again to avoid experiencing withdrawal.

Amy Williams, a twenty-two-year-old former spice addict, says that before she realized it, her body needed the drug in order to function. She explains:

> "You don't notice right away that you can't eat without smoking. Or that you can't sleep without it either. It's not until it's too late when you realize that your body is waking you up every three to four hours to get high."[41]
>
> —Amy Williams, a twenty-two-year-old former spice addict.

You don't notice right away that you can't eat without smoking. Or that you can't sleep without it either. It's not until it's too late when you realize that your body is waking you up every three to four hours to get high. . . . Eventually, all you think about is not running out, and when you do everything shuts down. It's impossible to eat because everything tastes like cardboard and most of it comes back up, violently.[41]

Addiction's Impact

Once addicted, the compelling desire to get high influences a person's decision making, often at the expense of other areas of life. Relationships can suffer if addicted users do not prioritize the needs of their partner, family, or friends. This is the case for an Australian woman who worries that synthetic marijuana is ruining her

Protective Factors Against Addiction

Although certain risk factors increase a person's chance of becoming addicted to synthetics, and any drug, there are several protective factors that can actually work to reduce one's potential for addiction. According to the NIDA, protective factors against addiction include having strong family bonds and being involved in social institutions such as school and religious organizations. In addition, a teen's relationship with his or her parents can be a protective factor. Teens whose parents are involved in their lives and monitor their friends and activities are less likely to use and become addicted to drugs. Being academically successful can also serve as a protective factor. The impact of each of these factors varies from person to person and can also vary according to a person's age. Prevention programs that strengthen protective factors in adolescents can thus be a critical tool in fighting addiction.

relationship with her partner. "Over the last five months I have noticed a large change in my partner's behavior," she told a reporter at the *Daily Mercury*, an Australian newspaper. "He has become paranoid, angry, not being involved with any family activities—slowly pushing his family and friends away."[42]

Addiction can also impede performance at work or at school. Many people who are addicted to synthetic drugs miss school or work because they are either getting high or experiencing withdrawal. Kinney, a young man from Tulsa, Oklahoma, says that his addiction to synthetic drugs such as K2 has ruined him financially. "It ruined my jobs. Every job I've ever had, it ruined it. It ruined my credit with my whole family. I'm in debt—total debt,"[43] he says. Despite this, Kinney does not know whether he will ever be able to stop using the drug.

Addicted users may also be arrested or face other legal trouble. Even though synthetics are technically legal, addicted users may act violently while high, get arrested, and serve jail time for their behavior. Addicts may also be arrested for stealing money or items to pay for drugs. In 2014, for example, three men from Linton, Indiana, were arrested for allegedly stealing checks, forging signatures, and cashing them to buy synthetic marijuana.

Risk Factors for Addiction

Like many other diseases, a lot of factors determine whether someone is vulnerable to addiction. Scientists believe there is no single factor that determines who will be prone to drug addiction. Instead, certain risk factors likely increase the chance that a person who uses drugs will become addicted.

Genes are one factor that determines a person's risk of developing addiction. Addiction is more common in some families than others. People with parents or siblings who are addicted to drugs or alcohol have an increased risk of becoming addicted themselves. According to the NIDA, scientists estimate that genetics account for between 40 and 60 percent of a person's risk of developing a drug addiction.

K2, a popular brand of synthetic marijuana, has been described by many as a sure path to ruin. Addicts lose everything—jobs, family, and friends—and often turn to crime to support their habit.

Environmental factors also come into play. Children raised in a home in which parents or older family members abuse alcohol or drugs are more likely to do so themselves. Teens who live in a chaotic or traumatic environment or who struggle at school may turn to drugs, including synthetics, in an effort to distract themselves from their problems. The social and school environments matter as well—teens who have friends who use drugs are also more likely to try drugs and, with regular use, become addicted.

> "Addiction, if left untreated, can—and often does—end in death."[46]
>
> —Marc Turner of the Greenhouse Treatment Center.

Age and frequency of use can also influence who becomes addicted to synthetic drugs. Although a person can become addicted at any age, those who start using synthetics as teens and those who use them daily are more likely to become addicted than those who start later in life and use them only occasionally. This factor may be the result of the harmful effect that synthetic drugs can have on the adolescent brain. Because the teen brain is still developing, introducing drugs that disrupt brain functioning at this critical time can have a lasting impact. Drugs that interfere with neurotransmitter function can damage developing neural connections. Use of synthetic drugs can also alter a teen's perception and interfere with developing perception skills. Repeated drug use may also become a habit that is ingrained in the teenage brain's wiring, making adolescents more susceptible to addiction.

The Devastating Consequences of Addiction

The long-term impact of synthetic drugs on the brain and body is not yet clear. To date, there has been limited research in this area. Because the chemical formulations are constantly changing, no one really knows what they contain. "When we buy these substances and send them to the lab, they could have one compound in it, or they could have five separate compounds,"[44] says

Overdose and Addiction

Amy Williams is a twenty-two-year-old student who used to be addicted to spice. She first began using it as a way to get high without failing a drug test. She describes what it was like when she overdosed, saying:

> I had lost complete control of myself. I was apparently rocking back and forth, which is common with overdoses on spice. I was incoherent and I felt like I was fighting something. I was fighting to get control of myself. I kept telling the two people I was with that I loved them. It was very important for them to know that because I thought I was going to die. My chest felt like it was caving in and I was shaking violently.

Despite her traumatic experience, Williams still feels the temptation of spice. "If it were in front of me I still don't think I have enough self-control to say no," she admits.

Quoted in Michelle Guerin, "Candid Confessions of a Spice Addict," Rehabs.com, April 7, 2014. www.rehabs.com.

John Scherbenske, who oversees the DEA's Synthetic Drugs and Chemicals Section. These differences make it very challenging to research and test the drugs' effects.

Although scientists are still learning about the damage synthetic drugs can cause, many users are aware of addiction's effects firsthand. For twenty-six-year-old Sylwia Wielgus from Poland, for example, years of synthetic drug use left her brain damaged. She used to smoke synthetic cannabinoids to cope with fighting with her parents and to escape other troubles in her home life. Now she has trouble remembering parts of her life. "I can't remember when I was 9, 10, 11 or 12," she says. "These drugs stole half of my life."[45] Not everyone who tries synthetic drugs will become addicted. But for some users, addiction can develop quickly and be devastating. As Marc Turner of the Greenhouse Treatment Center warns, "Addiction, if left untreated, can—and often does—end in death."[46]

CHAPTER 4: Challenges for Treatment and Recovery

Twenty-two-year-old Megan started smoking synthetic marijuana because she thought it was a legal way to get high—and she did not want to get arrested. She and her husband, Travis, smoked together, thinking that synthetic marijuana was a safe alternative to other drugs. Megan admits that she became addicted to the drug within eighteen months. When she tries to stop using it for less than a day, she trembles and cries. "I get the shakes, really hot. I can't focus on anything," she says. "When I get home . . . from work, the first thing I think about is smoking. I thought it was a safe alternative, so I jumped on the train. My husband and I work very hard. We're not bad people. We never figured we would have it this bad."[47]

Travis says his addiction causes him to prioritize synthetic marijuana over everything else in his life. He will take money intended for food and other necessities and spend it on drugs instead. "I've gone without toilet paper, but I had a bag of legal weed in this house," he says. "I've gone without food, but I had a bag of legal weed in this house. Instead of making the full payment (for utilities), we'd take the money and buy this stuff."[48]

Although they know they would be better off without synthetic marijuana, Megan and Travis admit that quitting is easier said than done. They are struggling to overcome their addiction to the drug. "This [drug] is highly addictive," Travis says. "I can kick (cigarettes) all day long . . . but this [drug] is something else."[49]

How to Treat Synthetic Drug Addiction

Addiction to synthetic drugs is complex but treatable. Because there are so many types of synthetic drugs and because all individuals are unique, no single treatment plan is appropriate for everyone. Instead, treatment and rehabilitation vary according to the type of drug that has been abused. Some synthetic drugs require longer treatment time than others, along with a more intense rehabilitation program. Most people benefit from a treatment program designed and administered by professionals.

A synthetic drug addiction is a chronic disease, like diabetes or heart disease. The sooner a patient seeks treatment, the better chance he or she will have of being able to kick the addiction. Dr. Sarah Wakeman runs the Substance Use Disorders Initiative at Massachusetts General Hospital, where doctors treat addiction as a chronic condition. Wakeman says that family and friends often struggle to view their loved one's problem as a chronic disease. "Your loved one with diabetes isn't going to rob you or steal from you," Wakeman says, "That can make it really hard for people to understand [addiction] as an illness."[50]

> "Your loved one with diabetes isn't going to rob you or steal from you. That can make it really hard for people to understand [addiction] as an illness."[50]
>
> —Dr. Sarah Wakeman, who runs the Substance Use Disorders Initiative at Massachusetts General Hospital.

Short-Term Treatment

Before addicts seek long-term treatment, they often require short-term treatment. Many first seek help in the emergency department because they are experiencing severe symptoms such as vomiting, rapid heartbeat, elevated blood pressure, seizures, hallucinations, extreme anxiety, or violent behavior. Synthetic drug use can confound hospital personnel in that they do not immediately know how to determine what a patient has taken. Synthetic drugs vary widely, as do their ingredients, which challenges first responders' ability to administer care. Synthetic drug users show up in emergency rooms with a wide range of bizarre symptoms, from becoming amorous to being angry and violent. "The people in the emergency rooms don't know what to test for," says Eric Wish, an associate professor and director of the Center for Substance Abuse Research at the University of Maryland. "It's a huge problem for public health."[51]

In some cases users who exhibit violent behavior can present a danger to hospital personnel. For example, people high on flakka act psychotically and aggressively and exhibit extraordinary strength. "Unlike a typical patient who requires one nurse, [patients using flakka] may require the assistance of three or four nurses, a doctor, a respiratory therapist, technicians and our police staff,"[52] says Christine Braud, an emergency room doctor who works for a hospital in Georgia. In one incident at Phoebe Putney Memorial Hospital in Albany, Georgia, a patient high on flakka attacked several staff members. The drug-crazed patient hit a nurse, attacked a security office with a chair, and caused extensive damage to hospital equipment. In cases like these, hospital staff members must sedate violent patients to prevent them from harming themselves and others.

Once such patients are sedated, doctors generally treat synthetic drug overdoses with antianxiety medications such as Valium or Xanax. These can calm the wild and uncontrolled activity in the patient's body and brain. "They cut back on the hallucinations, slow the heart rate, lower the blood pressure. It can take large doses. It can take repeated doses,"[53] says Dr. Elizabeth Scharman, director of the West Virginia Poison Center.

Other short-term treatments for synthetic drug abuse and overdose are symptom specific. Hospital staff members may administer medication to stop seizures or intubate a patient to support his or her airway. If a patient experiences chest pain, elevated blood pressure, or abnormal heart rate, doctors may order electrocardiogram tests and monitor cardiac functioning. Once a patient has been stabilized, he or she can begin the next phase of addiction recovery: withdrawal.

Getting Through Withdrawal

The first step to battling addiction is to endure withdrawal. A user's body has come to depend on the drug to function. Now, as the user attempts to quit, the body must return to a normal state and purge any traces of the drug and its toxins from the body. Though unpleasant, withdrawal symptoms are typically temporary. They usually begin a few hours after the last drug use and

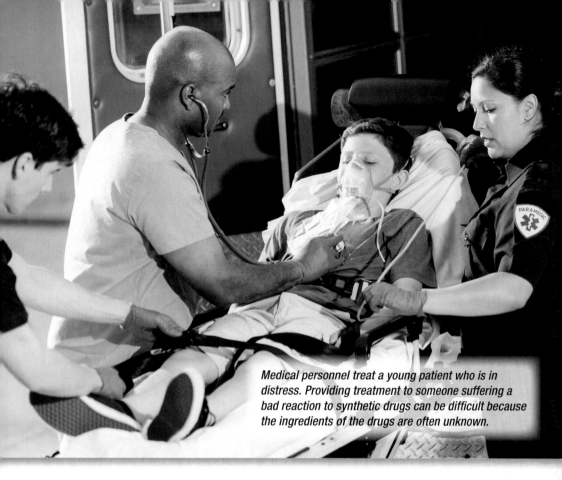

Medical personnel treat a young patient who is in distress. Providing treatment to someone suffering a bad reaction to synthetic drugs can be difficult because the ingredients of the drugs are often unknown.

can persist anywhere from a few days to a few weeks, depending on how long the patient has been using drugs.

The withdrawal process triggers a range of intense physical and psychological symptoms. People withdrawing from bath salts can experience insomnia, gastric distress, tremors, anxiety, paranoia, suicidal thoughts and behavior, psychotic behavior, delirium, and hallucinations. Patients withdrawing from synthetic marijuana may experience nightmares, irritability, anxiety, insomnia, lack of appetite, gastrointestinal difficulties, excessive sweating, headaches, dizziness, tremors, and chest pains. Addicts experiencing withdrawal may not be able to go to work or school for days as they battle extreme hangover- and flu-like symptoms.

In many cases these symptoms are too severe to handle alone. Users who try to quit on their own (that is, not in the context of a treatment program or not under a doctor's supervision) must handle withdrawal themselves, which is difficult. Some medications

Cognitive Behavioral Therapy

Cognitive behavioral therapy (CBT) is a form of psychotherapy used to treat synthetic drug addictions. CBT teaches patients skills that help them avoid drugs. These include strategies that help them identify and correct behaviors that led to drug use in the past, as well as ways to improve their self-control. For example, a patient may practice managing stress and anxiety with deep breathing and other relaxation techniques.

One of the core features of CBT is that it teaches patients how to anticipate situations that trigger drug use. When they find themselves in such situations, they are armed with coping strategies that do not involve using drugs. Patients learn to recognize drug cravings and identify high-risk situations where drug use is likely. They learn how to avoid these situations and deal with cravings without giving in to them.

can help people manage uncomfortable withdrawal symptoms, which may help them avoid relapsing. For example, antidepressant medications such as selective serotonin reuptake inhibitors may ease symptoms of anxiety. Other medications may reduce nausea and diarrhea or help a person sleep. These medications can be used to manage withdrawal symptoms for a few weeks until the symptoms cease.

In lieu of such help, however, people often relapse and use again, if only to make the withdrawal symptoms stop. This can sometimes lead to an overdose, which is when users take more of a drug than their body can handle. This is because during the withdrawal period, people's tolerance to the drug may have decreased. The same amount of spice or bath salt that got them high before they tried to quit may now be strong enough to cause a seizure or cardiac arrest. For this reason, it is extremely important that addicts receive medical supervision during the withdrawal process. Trained addiction recovery specialists monitor patients' progress and can administer medications to relieve withdrawal symptoms. They can also provide counseling and help with other issues that arise during withdrawal.

Although it is extremely difficult, some determined users have been able to handle quitting on their own. Brian, a single parent from Elkhart, Indiana, says that quitting synthetic marijuana was one of the hardest things he has ever done. He smoked synthetic marijuana for about six months before he decided to quit. He started out smoking a packet of synthetic marijuana called iBlown every week and a half. Within a few months, he was smoking a packet per day. Soon he started taking the drug to work with him so he could smoke when he felt sick. About four months into his habit, Brian realized he had to stop using the drug. "I knew I had to get off of it, with me being a single parent and being as involved in the community as I am," he says. "But I knew it was going to take days."[54]

He researched synthetic drugs and learned about the withdrawal process. He planned to quit cold turkey, taking some time off work and making sure his kids were with their mother. Withdrawal began the first night he stopped using the drug. "That night at three in the morning was when I started getting really sick," Brian says. "I couldn't sleep. From there on out, it was complete misery." For a few days, he stayed at home, feeling sick and

Withdrawal from synthetic drugs can be rough. Symptoms include tremors, anxiety, delirium, headaches, paranoia, dizziness, insomnia, irritability, and stomach upset.

unable to eat. He says it took him about two weeks to feel physically normal and about a month to feel mentally sound. "I had to really think hard to do some of the simplest things," he says. "When I started reading about [withdrawing from synthetics] they said it was the equivalent to heroin. I've never done hard drugs, I have no idea what it's like, but I know coming off this fake stuff is unreal."[55]

Inpatient and Outpatient Rehabilitation

Ridding the body of all traces of synthetic drugs is just the first step in recovery. Without additional treatment, the patient is likely to relapse and start using drugs again. The right treatment program depends on the severity of the person's addiction and whether he or she has any co-occurring issues such as a mood disorder, an eating disorder, or another substance abuse problem.

Patients with a severe addiction or one complicated by the presence of a co-occurring disorder often need to be placed in an inpatient residential treatment program. Inpatient programs provide a more immersive, time-intensive treatment experience than at-home treatment affords. Inpatient programs remove people from the circumstances that enabled their addiction. When they are no longer exposed to the people and environment that led to drug use, they can work more productively toward addiction recovery.

> "That night at three in the morning was when I started getting really sick. I couldn't sleep. From there on out, it was complete misery."[55]
>
> —Brian, an addict describing withdrawing from synthetic drugs.

For most people an inpatient residential program lasts thirty days, during which they live in a supervised facility. Most inpatient stays begin with an initial assessment, in which mental health professionals determine the nature of the patient's addiction and if there are any co-occurring mental health disorders. The facility will also help the patient withdraw from bath salts, spice, or other synthetic drugs. Medical professionals monitor the patient, providing support and care as needed to help manage withdrawal symptoms. Patients also participate in group and individual ther-

12-Step Programs

Narcotics Anonymous (NA) is a treatment program modeled after Alcoholics Anonymous. Membership is open to anyone trying to overcome drug or alcohol dependence. In the program, new members are assigned a sponsor who has been clean for at least a year. This person helps recovering addicts deal with cravings and challenges as they occur. NA helps members recover from addiction by walking them through a 12-step process. As a first step, addicts admit that they are powerless to stop using drugs and that they have a problem. Members work through the following steps, which include thinking about decisions they have made and making amends to people their addictive behavior has harmed. Although NA is not affiliated with any specific religion, it is considered by some to be a spiritual support and recovery program.

NA members regularly attend meetings, where they listen to speakers, participate in group discussions, study literature, and celebrate staying clean. Some meetings are restricted to recovering addicts, whereas others welcome nonaddicts who want to support a loved one or learn more about addiction. In an NA 2013 Membership Survey, members say that attending meetings has improved several areas of their lives, including family relationships and social connections.

apy sessions, where they learn how to develop healthy coping skills and to deal with and change the negative thoughts and behaviors that led to drug use.

Addicts with more serious needs may stay in an inpatient rehabilitation program for sixty or even ninety days, or a length of time customized to their needs. After the inpatient portion of the treatment program, patients typically enroll in aftercare programs that include additional therapy and support groups. Support groups help addicts deal with the daily challenges of living without drugs. Recovering addicts can talk about their progress and challenges with other patients who are struggling with the same issues. Other group members can provide valuable support and advice. In these environments, patients practice strengthening the skills they learned while in rehab that help prevent relapse.

People suffering from a milder synthetic drug addiction may choose to attend an outpatient rehabilitation program. Outpatient treatment programs allow patients to live at home while receiving treatment. This option works well for those who need to maintain responsibilities at work, school, and home. Intensive outpatient treatment programs meet initially for three to four days per week for two to four hours per session. They often feature individual and group counseling and focus on preventing relapse. Group counseling involves attending a session with other addicts that is led by a trained therapist. At each session, participants discuss issues of addiction and recovery with people who are going through the same experience. During individual counseling, patients meet one-on-one with a trained therapist to identify their personal causes of addiction and learn tailored coping skills to deal with the issues that led to their drug use.

Barriers to Recovery

Several barriers make it difficult for addicts to achieve long-term recovery. One is the belief that synthetic drugs are safe. Because many users believe they cannot get addicted to synthetics, many are unwilling to admit they have a problem. Jim Yonai, the Mental Health Department director in Madison County, New York, says that despite the growing number of people who have had extreme reactions to bath salts and synthetic marijuana, only a few users participate in treatment. For example, Yonai says that although dozens of bath salt users treated in local emergency rooms in 2012 were referred to Madison County's drug treatment programs, only two enrolled in a program.

The availability of synthetic drugs is another significant barrier to addiction recovery. Addicts can simply walk down the street to the nearest gas station and buy more, making relapse tempting and more likely. This has been difficult for Shelby Nordstrom, a recovering addict from Minnesota who attends a 12-step addiction treatment program. Nordstrom says that he struggles daily with temptation. "It's so easy to get it," he says. "And that's the hard part, you know?"[56]

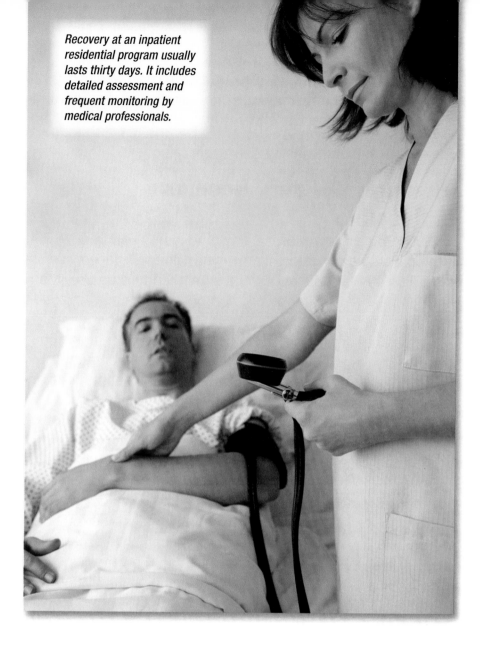

Recovery at an inpatient residential program usually lasts thirty days. It includes detailed assessment and frequent monitoring by medical professionals.

Making recovery further challenging is the fact that some people who abuse synthetic drugs do so to deal with an undiagnosed mental illness. According to Promises Treatment Centers, which specializes in addiction treatment for a wide range of substances, "More than half the people struggling with drug addiction suffer from a co-occurring mental health disorder such as depression, chronic anxiety, bipolar disorder, or another personality disorder."[57] For these users, synthetic drugs are a cheap and easy way to self-medicate and escape their problems. Without receiving a diagnosis for an underlying mental health condition, the same issues that drove the addict to use in the first place will resurface during the recovery process. When this happens, the likelihood of relapse is high.

Although Difficult, Recovery Is Possible

Addiction is a chronic disease. It can be terrifically difficult to stay clean once a person returns to everyday life and is faced with the pressures and circumstances that initially led to drug use. Many patients need a long-term-care approach that is customized to their changing needs.

For twenty-one-year-old Hanna, the road to recovering from a bath salt addiction has been long and difficult. At the height of her addiction, the drugs almost ruined her life. "I thought I was demonized and possessed at one point. I would scratch and slash at myself. I would be thrown back, and I would try to snap my own neck," she says. "It's so scary because I don't even know why it was so addicting to me, but I had to just keep doing it." Hanna experienced intense hallucinations while high. She would hide in her room and be unable to sleep because she was terrified of the demons she saw. "And then it slowly turned into voices," she explains. "It was just constant, it never stopped."[58]

After fourteen months, Hanna realized she needed help. "I never thought that any kind of substance could control my life the way bath salts ended up controlling it," she says. She entered an inpatient rehabilitation program near her home and continues to receive daily outpatient care. Today she is drug free and has left behind the demons. Of addiction to synthetic drugs, she warns, "It can happen to anybody. I was doing just fine. I was brought up very well, and it completely consumed me," she says. "It's such a horrific and terrifying drug."[59]

> "I never thought that any kind of substance could control my life the way bath salts ended up controlling it."[59]
>
> —Hanna, a twenty-one-year-old former synthetic drug addict.

CHAPTER 5: Preventing Synthetic Drug Use

Because of the harm synthetic drugs cause, law enforcement, heath care officials, and users' families and friends argue it is critical to prevent their use. Prevention typically takes three forms. One is making these substances illegal; another is making it harder to make and buy them; and another is educating the public and retailers about the dangers of their use.

Laws to Ban Synthetic Drugs

A main reason people choose to use synthetic drugs is because they are legal and easy to buy. Recognizing this, the government has taken steps to ban synthetics. On July 9, 2012, President Barack Obama signed the Synthetic Drug Abuse Prevention Act into law. It permanently places twenty-six types of synthetic cannabinoids and cathinones into Schedule I of the Controlled Substances Act. This act regulates drugs' manufacture, possession, use, and distribution according to five "schedules," of which Schedule I drugs are the most dangerous. Mephedrone and MDPV, which are used to make bath salts, were also listed as Schedule I drugs, placing them in the same category as heroin and LSD. "President Obama's swift approval of this federal ban is the final nail in the coffin for the legal sale of bath salts in smoke shops and convenience stores in New York State and throughout the rest of the country," said Senator Charles Schumer of New York. "This law will close loopholes . . . and ensure that you cannot simply cross state lines to find these deadly bath salts."[60]

States have taken action too. Since 2011 all fifty states have banned two types of synthetic drugs—cannabinoids and cathinones. The majority of state laws initially targeted specific versions of the drugs by issuing individual bans on specific chemical formulas. This type of legislation added certain substances to states' controlled substance schedules. Banned synthetic cannabinoids include JWH-018, HU-210, and CP 47,497. Banned synthetic cathinones include mephedrone, MDPV, methylone, and methedrone.

In response to the individual bans, synthetic drug manufacturers have simply made minor changes to drug formulas. They do this by using new ingredients that are not (yet) on states' controlled substance schedules. These new but very similar drugs are not covered by the laws and thus are not technically illegal. "The formulas of the synthetic drugs are constantly being changed to stay a step ahead of law enforcement,"[61] explains the Washington, DC US Attorney's Office. Sherry Green, CEO of the National Alliance for Model State Drug Laws, has put this problem in perspective by saying, "States find they have to play catch-up."[62] In October 2011, for example, state lawmakers in Ohio passed legislation to ban synthetic drugs, but chemists maneuvered around the law by altering the products' chemical components. "Clever chemists stayed a step ahead of us," says Ohio attorney general Mike DeWine. "By just tweaking the recipe—adding several molecules here or changing several molecules there—chemists create a brand new drug."[63]

"The formulas of the synthetic drugs are constantly being changed to stay a step ahead of law enforcement."[61]

—Washington, DC, US Attorney's Office in a 2015 statement.

To address this issue, several states have tried to pass more general legislation that aims to ban multiple varieties of synthetic drugs, rather than individual formulas. General bans target entire classes of substances or use broad language to describe a drug. Some laws describe a general chemical makeup, whereas others use chemical classes to describe groupings of similar synthetics. In this way, general bans aim to prevent new forms of synthetics from going unregulated by outlawing a class of substances, and then giving specific examples of substances within that class. "If something else in that class is created after the law takes effect, it would already be banned,"[64] explains Green.

Drug Enforcement Administration technicians test the chemical makeup of confiscated synthetic drugs. These drugs are a moving target because drug makers are constantly changing their formulas and ingredients.

In 2012 Ohio passed a general law banning synthetic drugs, closing a loophole in its previous ban that effectively allowed synthetic drug makers to keep selling their products. "The synthetic drug problem is constantly evolving, and we can't afford to risk falling behind,"[65] said DeWine of his state's efforts. Ohio's new law gives law enforcement a wider net to catch manufacturers, distributors, and users of synthetic drugs. It bans whole classes of synthetic cannabinoids, along with many 2C compounds, which are a type of psychedelic drug. It also bans an entire class of compounds used in bath salts. In November 2012 the Ohio attorney general sent a letter to retailers to advise them of the changes. "Some store owners and employees continue to sell these drugs under the table, despite knowing how dangerous they are," says DeWine. "Anyone who sells or distributes these drugs should be prepared for both criminal charges and a civil lawsuit."[66]

Some states have passed what are called analogue laws to combat the synthetic drug industry. Analogue laws ban drugs that are not classified as controlled substances but are very similar to

Project Synergy

In October 2015 the DEA announced it had arrested 151 people in sixteen states on charges related to the synthetic drug industry. The DEA also seized more than $15 million in cash and drugs. The arrests were part of Project Synergy III, a joint investigation by the DEA, Immigration and Customs Enforcement, Homeland Security Investigations, and several other federal, state, and local law enforcement agencies. Project Synergy III was a fifteen-month, nationwide effort to target the synthetic drug industry and its manufacturers, wholesalers, and retailers.

Previous phases of Project Synergy identified and targeted consignment shipments coming into the United States that were suspected to contain synthetic drugs. "Shutting down businesses that traffic in these drugs and attacking their operations worldwide is a priority for DEA and our law enforcement partners," says DEA administrator Michele Leonhart. The first phase of Project Synergy, which began in December 2012, resulted in more than 416 search warrants and 227 arrests in 35 states. Agents seized more than $51 million in cash and assets, including 10.4 tons (9.4 metric tons) of individually packaged synthetic drugs.

Quoted in US Drug Enforcement Administration, "Updated Results from DEA's Largest-Ever Global Synthetic Drug Takedown Yesterday," June 26, 2013. www.dea.gov.

ones that have already been prohibited. Generally, these laws ban drugs that are substantially alike in chemical structure and have a similar effect on the central nervous system as an already scheduled controlled substance. An example of a state that has passed analogue laws is Alabama, which in 2014 passed two new laws that banned about 160 synthetic drug recipes. The new legislation will help prosecute cases that involve drugs that are slightly different than illegal drugs but achieve a similar effect.

However, critics of analogue laws say that in some legal trials, prosecutors have had difficulty winning these cases because there is often not enough scientific research on the substance's chemical structure or its effect on the body to provide significant evidence in court. And beyond analogue laws, others are skeptical of the extent to which legislation is able to prevent or reduce synthetic drug use. Anthony Tambasco, a forensic scientist in Mansfield, Ohio, believes that new synthetic drug compounds will continue be created despite new laws. He expects synthetic drug manufacturers will eventually find new ways to get around legislation. "They're already out in front of it," he says. "They're already on their next batch."[67]

Creative Strategies to Combat the Synthetic Drug Industry

Other states have taken different approaches to regulate and prevent synthetic drug use. These include changing who has the authority to ban a substance, modifying consumer protection laws, and using existing laws to stop drug sales.

To keep up with the quickly changing synthetic drug market, states have delegated, or given, the authority to ban substances to pharmacy boards or other agencies that can act more quickly than the state legislature. Passing laws takes time; a bill must be drafted, debated, and passed through committees and both houses of a state legislature and approved by the state's governor. This process can take months or even years. Therefore, some state legislatures have authorized other agencies—which are not subject to the above processes—to pass temporary bans on substances, which are later reviewed and approved by the legislature. An example of a state that has adopted this strategy is Minnesota, which in 2012 authorized its Board of Pharmacy to temporarily add substances to a controlled substance schedule. The Minnesota legislature later reviewed these additions and approved them. Similarly, in New York the legislature authorized the commissioner of the Department of Health to make permanent rules and regulations for the good of public health. The commissioner used this authority to ban the manufacture, sale, and use of many synthetic drugs.

Some states have also passed laws that restrict synthetic drug–related marketing, displays, labeling, and advertising. Many synthetic drugs are marketed as bath salts, herbal incense, potpourri, or other types of products that they are not qualified to be called. They are also labeled "not for human consumption," despite the fact that the people who make and sell these drugs are aware that their products are consumed to get high. "Everyone knows these are drugs to get high [with], including the sellers,"[68] says Barbara Carreno, a spokesperson for the DEA. Given this, states are using consumer protection, product labeling, and branding laws to prosecute those who sell synthetics. These are laws that protect consumers from unsafe or deceptively labeled or packaged products.

For example, Illinois has put criminal penalties in place for falsely advertising or misbranding synthetic drugs as products that they are, in reality, not. Similarly, in 2012 the New York state attorney general used this idea to file a lawsuit against twelve retailers that sell synthetic cannabinoids and cathinones. The state argued that the retailers violated state labeling laws because they did not include manufacturing information, product content, and safety and health risks associated with product use. The state also alleged that the retailers violated labeling laws by marking the products "not for human consumption," when in reality that is their intended purpose. The lawsuit further asserts that the retailers acted fraudulently and deceptively.

In 2013 New York Supreme Court justice James McClusky issued a decision in one of these lawsuits that John Tebbetts III, the owner of eight shops in New York, was responsible for selling deceptively labeled drug products. The court's order permanently bans the sale of any misbranded or mislabeled drugs. "Judge McClusky has seen through the fraud being perpetrated by the industry, and his ruling will be another important tool in dismantling an insidious growth of illicit over the counter drug sales within our communities," said New York attorney general Eric Schneiderman. "The judge's order proves that, by taking a creative approach in using the state's existing labeling laws, we can get swift results to remove dangerous drugs from store shelves and hold sellers accountable for breaking the law."[69]

Finally, in yet another creative approach, some states are using agricultural regulations to prosecute synthetic drug manufacturers and distributors. Since some synthetic cathinones are often marketed as plant food, states like Tennessee are prosecuting distributors under agricultural regulations that require all fertilizers to be registered with the commissioner of agriculture before distribution.

Teen Use of Synthetic Marijuana Is Declining

Efforts to educate adolescents about synthetic drugs appear to be having a positive impact. The percentage of eighth-, tenth-, and twelfth-grade students reporting they had used synthetic cannabinoids in the past twelve months has declined since 2012.

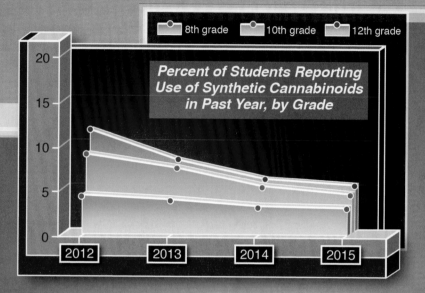

Source: National Institute on Drug Abuse, 2015 Monitoring the Future Survey, December 2015. www.drugabuse.gov.

Public Education

In addition to legislation, public education is a critical part of preventing synthetic drug use. Educating people of all ages about the risks of these drugs is a natural way to prevent their use. To this end, government agencies, local communities, schools, and grassroots organizations are all working to enlighten the public.

The federal government has created educational materials that focus specifically on synthetic drugs. For example, the Office of National Drug Control Policy has developed a synthetic drugs information kit that includes a slide cast, podcast, and video that teaches about the effects of synthetic drugs. The kit also includes a parents' guide that lists the different street names of the drugs and describes signs of their use, along with a tip sheet that helps parents communicate with and monitor their children.

States are also working to educate their citizens. In Florida, for example, the state attorney general and the Department of Law Enforcement developed a synthetic drug information pamphlet that contains information about synthetic drugs and applicable laws in Florida. Meanwhile, in 2015 New York responded to a significant increase in synthetic drug–related emergency room visits by launching two public service announcements (PSAs). The PSAs feature young adults warning people not to use synthetic drugs, and the ads aired on television and music streaming services across the state. "These PSAs spread the simple message that these drugs are harmful, addictive, and simply not worth it,"[70] says New York governor Andrew Cuomo. New York also created a 33-foot (10 m) billboard in the Bronx that warns about synthetic marijuana. Similar posters will be placed in subways, bus shelters, and other locations around New York City, and billboards will go up at malls around the state. "New York State is at a crossroads," says Arlene Gonzalez-Sanchez, commissioner of the Office of Alcoholism and Substance Abuse Services. "Now is the time to stamp out synthetics."[71]

> "These PSAs spread the simple message that these drugs are harmful, addictive, and simply not worth it."[70]
>
> —Andrew Cuomo, the governor of New York.

Local communities and schools have partnered to develop programs that educate students about the risks of synthetics. In Tennessee, for example, police officers have gone into schools to teach students about the risks and dangers of synthetics. Officers met with students and talked to them about the side effects of synthetic drugs. They also told them that medical personnel face many challenges in treating people who have used bath salts or synthetic marijuana.

The program has apparently met with success. "I knew they were legal, but I didn't know how bad they were or how much people were affected by [them],"[72] says Jennifer Brewer, a freshman at David Crockett High School who attended the program. According to Sheriff Ed Graybeal, these programs reach students before they encounter such drugs on the street. "The more education we put out there, the more power these students are going

Undercover: Buying Synthetic Drugs

Despite the growing illegality of synthetic drugs, many stores continue to sell them. In 2012 investigative journalists for CBS went undercover to find stores in the Atlanta area that were still selling bath salts, even though these substances have been banned by the state of Georgia. When one undercover journalist asked if he could buy bath salts at a smoke shop called Smoke 911, the cashier told him no but said that the shop carried the "bubbling stuff" instead. When asked, the cashier explained that it was different than bath salts.

Later, journalists confronted the store about the illegal sale. "Are you sure you're not selling bath salts?" asked reporter Steve Kiggins. The cashier denied it. "We actually bought some of those today," said Kiggins. The cashier continued to deny that he had sold bath salts and demanded that the news team leave the store. According to Lance Dyer, whose son committed suicide after using synthetic marijuana, it is unconscionable that stores like Smoke 911 continue to sell synthetics even though they are banned. "They know what they're selling is illegal, they know what they're selling is poisonous," says Dyer.

Quoted in CBS46.com, "Undercover: Synthetic Drugs Still Selling at Area Smoke Shops," July 27, 2012. www.cbs46.com.

to have to make the right decision when they come across this stuff,"[73] he says. Students like freshman Aaron Ford think the program is making a difference. "Where the drugs themselves are so scary, just knowing the facts, it definitely scared a lot of people. It scared me off from even thinking about it,"[74] says Ford.

Grassroots organizations are also acting to prevent synthetic drug use. Many such organizations came into being after a tragedy. For example, after David Rozga smoked K2 and committed suicide, his family launched K2 Drug Facts. This website provides facts and resources about synthetic drugs, as well as news about current legislation. The Rozga family hopes the site will increase public knowledge about synthetic drug dangers. The Rozgas believe that if their son had known the risks, he would have never tried K2.

Jan and Mike Rozga and their son Daniel display a photo of David Rozga, who committed suicide after smoking K2. In hopes of increasing public awareness, the Rozgas have created a website that provides the hard facts about synthetic drugs.

Another grassroots organization, the To the Maximus Foundation, was similarly founded by the family of a young man who died after using synthetic marijuana. At the time, nineteen-year-old Max Dobner told a friend that the drug must be safe because it was legal. Today the foundation partners with the media to educate the public about the risks of synthetics and advocates for legislation to ban synthetic drugs. Such organizations exist not just in the United States, but around the world. In New Zealand, for example, thirty-nine-year-old Julie King has organized a grassroots protest in twenty-two towns across the country aimed at synthetic drugs. King is a former addict who feels it is her duty to speak out against the sale and distribution of synthetic drugs.

Involving Retailers in Prevention

As coverage of synthetic drugs' serious effects grows, some retail associations have joined the fight against them. In June 2012, for example, the Michigan Food and Beverage Association, which represents thirty-five hundred Michigan party stores and gas stations where synthetics are often sold, adopted a no-sale policy for synthetic marijuana and also supported legislation that banned the drugs. "This is a deadly and dangerous family of products, which do not belong for sale anywhere, much less on store shelves," said Jennifer Kluge, the association's president and chief executive officer. "We certainly do not want to see these products at any of our member merchant locations."[75] Also in 2012, the Georgia Association of Convenience Stores asked member stores not to sell synthetic drug products.

> "The more education we put out there, the more power these students are going to have to make the right decision when they come across this stuff."[73]
>
> —Ed Graybeal, the sheriff in Washington County, Tennessee.

After the Synthetic Drug Abuse Prevention Act of 2012 was passed, the National Association of Convenience Stores warned its approximately 148,000 member stores to take these products off shelves. Mustafa Jamal, who owns a Sunoco gas station and convenience store in Richmond, Virginia, says he immediately removed synthetics from his store. "The day it was banned, the entire thing was thrown out of the building,"[76] says Jamal. He admits that manufacturers of synthetic products still approach him about carrying products in his store, but he turns them down because he does not want to break the law.

Some national convenience store chains have committed to getting spice, K2, and other synthetic drugs off store shelves. In June 2012, BP, a large oil company, sent a letter to local gas station owners requiring them to stop all sales of spice and similar products. BP's Susan Hayden wrote in the letter:

> Beginning immediately, all BP-branded sites are prohibited from displaying, using, storing, offering or selling illegal drugs, or synthetic drugs produced to mimic illegal drugs, (including, but not limited to cannabinoids), or items that are intended or designed for use in ingesting, inhaling or otherwise consuming an illegal drug. Prohibited items will include, but not be limited to, pipes, tubes, roach clips, instructions or descriptive materials, or containers for concealing illegal drugs or paraphernalia.[77]

Other stores have responded to orders from the government. In 2015, for example, the attorneys general of forty-three states sent a letter to several major oil companies, including Shell, Citgo, ExxonMobil, and Chevron, asking them to ensure that synthetic drugs are banned from retail sites bearing their name. They also asked the companies to revoke a franchise—that is, to cancel their corporate affiliation—with any gas station or convenience store caught selling these products. "We urge these companies to remove these dangerous products from store shelves and ensure that they are no longer available in any branded gas station or convenience store,"[78] said Massachusetts attorney general Maura Healey.

Even so, many independently owned stores continue to market synthetic drug products, even after the substances are banned. The products might be kept under the counter or in a drawer and only brought out if the customer knows what to ask for. Merchants face arrest and prosecution for selling synthetic drugs illegally. In February 2015, for example, police busted Thamer Jarjees, the owner of a Las Vegas convenience store, for selling spice. Jarjees had already been warned twice that it was illegal to sell the dangerous drug. During a search of the store, police found 24 pounds (11 kg) of spice behind the front counter and in a back office. Jarjees admitted that he sold the drug to customers who asked for incense. He used a separate cash register for spice sales. Then, at the end of the day, Jarjees would take the money from the spice register and put it into the main register, ringing up false grocery purchases to account for it. For his actions, Jarjees faces two felony charges of trafficking a controlled substance.

Prevention Efforts Are Working

Through a combination of legislation, education, and law enforcement activity, progress is being made toward reducing synthetic drug use. According to the NIDA's 2015 Monitoring the Future survey, the use of synthetic cannabinoids by high school seniors has declined—5.2 percent of twelfth graders reported using synthetic marijuana in the past year, which was a significant drop from the 11.4 percent recorded in 2011. Although current prevention and education efforts are working to reduce synthetic drug use, more efforts are needed. In particular, prevention efforts aimed at kids before they ever use synthetics are critical.

SOURCE NOTES

Chapter 1: What Are Synthetic Drugs?

1. Quoted in Antoinette Konz and Tamara Evans, "Undercover Investigation: Dangerous Synthetic Drugs Sold to Teens at Louisville Shops," WDRB.com, October 21, 2015. www.wdrb.com.
2. Quoted in Konz and Evans, "Undercover Investigation."
3. Quoted in Christina Zdanowicz, "Teen Narrowly Escapes Death After Smoking Synthetic Marijuana," CNN, February 5, 2013. www.cnn.com.
4. Quoted in Judy Woodruff, "What's in the Synthetic Drug? An Unknown Grab-Bag of Toxic Chemicals," video, *PBS NewsHour*, December 22, 2015. www.pbs.org.
5. Quoted in Jenny Marder, "The Drug That Never Lets Go," *PBS NewsHour*, September 20, 2012. www.pbs.org.
6. Quoted in Alice G. Walton, "Why Synthetic Marijuana Is More Toxic to the Brain than Pot," *Forbes*, August 28, 2014. www.forbes.com.
7. Quoted in Tisha Thompson, "What 'Synthetic Drugs' Really Look Like," NBC Washington, August 27, 2015. www.nbcwashington.com.
8. Quoted in Thompson, "What 'Synthetic Drugs' Really Look Like."
9. Quoted in Deborah Brauser, "New Deadly Class of Synthetic Hallucinogens Mimics LSD," Medscape, December 10, 2014. www.medscape.com.
10. Quoted in J.J. Hensley, "'N-bomb' Drug Stirs Fear Among Police, Doctors," *USA Today*, May 4, 2013. www.usatoday.com.
11. Quoted in Drew Griffin and Nelli Black, "Deadly High: How Synthetic Drugs Are Killing Kids," CNN, December 2, 2014. www.cnn.com.

12. Quoted in Carina Storrs, "What Is Flakka (aka Gravel) and Why Is It More Dangerous than Cocaine?," CNN, May 26, 2015. www.cnn.com.
13. Quoted in Storrs, "What Is Flakka (aka Gravel) and Why Is It More Dangerous than Cocaine?"
14. Quoted in Hensley, "'N-bomb' Drug Stirs Fear Among Police, Doctors."
15. Quoted in Stephen Stock and David Paredes, "The Law Has Trouble Keeping Up with Synthetic Drugs," NBC Bay Area, February 13, 2014. www.nbcbayarea.com.

Chapter 2: Effects of Synthetic Drug Use

16. Quoted in Griffin and Black, "Deadly High."
17. Quoted in Walton, "Why Synthetic Marijuana Is More Toxic to the Brain than Pot."
18. Quoted in Walton, "Why Synthetic Marijuana Is More Toxic to the Brain than Pot."
19. Quoted in Walton, "Why Synthetic Marijuana Is More Toxic to the Brain than Pot."
20. Quoted in Marder, "The Drug That Never Lets Go."
21. Quoted in Marder, "The Drug That Never Lets Go."
22. Quoted in Dan Rankin, "Synthetic Marijuana 'Spice' Linked to Stroke," Medscape, January 21, 2014. www.medscape.com.
23. Quoted in Jamie Lampros, "Abuse of Synthetic Drugs Rises, More Teens Hospitalized," *Ogden (UT) Standard-Examiner*, August 1, 2015. www.standard.net.
24. Quoted in Dennis Thompson, "New Synthetic Drug 'Flakka' Triggers Crazed Behaviors," HealthDay, April 16, 2015. http://consumer.healthday.com.
25. Quoted in Gillian Mohney, "Calls to Poison Control Centers Linked to Synthetic Marijuana Spike 229%, CDC Says," ABC News, June 11, 2015. http://abcnews.go.com.
26. Quoted in Alan Schwarz, "Potent 'Spice' Drug Fuels Rise in Visits to Emergency Room," *New York Times*, April 24, 2015. www.nytimes.com.

27. Quoted in Lampros, "Abuse of Synthetic Drugs Rises, More Teens Hospitalized."

28. Quoted in Zdanowicz, "Teen Narrowly Escapes Death After Smoking Synthetic Marijuana."

29. Quoted in Bridget Ortigo, "Texas Teen Speaks Against Using Synthetic Marijuana," *Longview (TX) News-Journal*, May 28, 2015. www.news-journal.com.

30. Quoted in Ortigo, "Texas Teen Speaks Against Using Synthetic Marijuana."

31. Quoted in Ortigo, "Texas Teen Speaks Against Using Synthetic Marijuana."

32. Quoted in Celia Vimont, "States Look for New Way to Fight Synthetic Drugs," Partnership for Drug-Free Kids, November 19, 2013. www.drugfree.org.

Chapter 3: How Addictive Are Synthetic Drugs?

33. Quoted in Erin Holt, "Former Synthetic Drug Addict Speaks to H.S. Students," WKRN News 2, November 15, 2011. http://wkrn.com.

34. Quoted in Holt, "Former Synthetic Drug Addict Speaks to H.S. Students."

35. Quoted in Alice G. Walton, "Synthetic Drug 'Bath Salts' Trumps Methamphetamine in Addictiveness, Study Finds," *Forbes*, July 10, 2013. www.forbes.com.

36. Quoted in Scripps Research Institute, "TSRI Scientists Find Hyped New Recreational Drug 'Flakka' Is as Addictive as Bath Salts," May 8, 2015. www.scripps.edu.

37. Quoted in Carol Ferguson, "Mothers Speak of Horrifying Effect of Spice Drug: 'He Throws Up Blood,'" Bakersfield Now .com, April 29, 2013. http://bakersfieldnow.com.

38. Quoted in Letisha Bush, "Spice Addict Speaks Out, Warns Users," Fox10TV.com, April 22, 2014. www.fox10tv.com.

39. Quoted in Sharon Tay, "Woman, 21, Shares Her Struggle to Overcome Addiction to Bath Salts," CBS Los Angeles, October 26, 2012. http://losangeles.cbslocal.com.

40. Quoted in Scripps Research Institute, "TSRI Scientists Find Hyped New Recreational Drug 'Flakka' Is as Addictive as Bath Salts."

41. Quoted in Michelle Guerin, "Candid Confessions of a Spice Addict," Rehabs.com, April 7, 2014. www.rehabs.com.

42. Quoted in Chris Lees, "'Fake' Drugs Ruin Lives," *Daily Mercury* (Mackay, Queensland, Australia), November 1, 2014. www .dailymercury.com.au.

43. Quoted in Lacie Lowry, "Green Country Man Speaks About Synthetic Marijuana Addiction," NewsOn6.com, November 27, 2012. www.newson6.com.

44. Quoted in Tricia Escobedo, "What You Need to Know About Synthetic Drugs," CNN, September 13, 2013. www.cnn.com.

45. Quoted in Joanna Berendt, "Poisonings in Poland Illustrate Global Challenge of Synthetic Drugs," *New York Times*, October 14, 2015. www.nytimes.com.

46. Quoted in Rebecca Lopez, "Flakka: Dangerous, Addictive Drug Comes to North Texas," WFAA.com, July 13, 2015. www.wfaa.com.

Chapter 4: Challenges for Treatment and Recovery

47. Quoted in Fred Hiers, "The Dangers and Addiction of 'Fake' Marijuana," *Ocala (FL) Star-Banner*, April 14, 2012. www.oc ala.com.

48. Quoted in Hiers, "The Dangers and Addiction of 'Fake' Marijuana."

49. Quoted in Hiers, "The Dangers and Addiction of 'Fake' Marijuana."

50. Quoted in Martha Bebinger, "No Blame, No Shame: Treating Heroin Addiction as a Chronic Condition," CommonHealth, September 9, 2015. http://commonhealth.wbur.org.

51. Quoted in Elizabeth Whitman, "'Spice' Drug Effects: Synthetic Marijuana Unpredictably Dangerous, Even Deadly, Experts Say, as Hospitalizations Rise," *International Business Times*, April 28, 2015. www.ibtimes.com.

52. Quoted in Zack Winn, "Why Flakka Patients Are Creating Security Risks for Hospitals," *Campus Safety*, February 16, 2016. www.campussafetymagazine.com.

53. Quoted in Jim Salter and Jim Suhr, "Synthetic Drugs Send Thousands to the ER," NBC News, April 6, 2011. www.nbc news.com.

54. Quoted in Sharon Hernandez, "Former User Shares Personal Synthetic Marijuana Withdrawal Experience," *Elkhart (IN) Truth*, June 14, 2014. www.elkharttruth.com.

55. Quoted in Hernandez, "Former User Shares Personal Synthetic Marijuana Withdrawal Experience."

56. Quoted in KBJR News 1, "Synthetic Drug Addiction: A Real-Life Perspective," NNCNOW.com, April 4, 2013. www.north landsnewscenter.com.

57. Promises Treatment Centers, "Top Reasons Men in Recovery Relapse with Drugs," January 21, 2013. www.promises.com.

58. Quoted in Tay, "Woman, 21, Shares Her Struggle to Overcome Addiction to Bath Salts."

59. Quoted in Tay, "Woman, 21, Shares Her Struggle to Overcome Addiction to Bath Salts."

Chapter 5: Preventing Synthetic Drug Use

60. Quoted in Nok-Noi Ricker, "President Signs Federal Synthetic Bath Salts Ban," *Bangor (ME) Daily News*, July 14, 2012. http://bangordailynews.com.

61. Quoted in Peter Hermann, "Difficulties Testing Synthetic Drugs Are Slowing Criminal Prosecutions," *Washington Post*, July 10, 2015. www.washingtonpost.com.

62. Quoted in Vimont, "States Look for New Way to Fight Synthetic Drugs."

63. Quoted in Ohio Attorney General, "New Weapons Take Aim at Synthetic Drugs," January 23, 2013. www.ohioattorney general.gov.

64. Quoted in Vimont, "States Look for New Way to Fight Synthetic Drugs."

65. Quoted in Ohio Attorney General, "New Weapons Take Aim at Synthetic Drugs."

66. Quoted in Ohio Attorney General, "New Weapons Take Aim at Synthetic Drugs."

67. Quoted in Partnership for Drug-Free Kids, "Federal Law Banning Synthetic Drugs May Not Be Effective, Some Experts Say," July 12, 2012. www.drugfree.org.

68. Quoted in CBS News, "Many Synthetic Drugs Still Legal After 'Bath Salts' Ban," July 25, 2012. www.cbsnews.com.

69. Quoted in Brian Cohen, "N.Y. AG Wins Case Banning Sale of Mislabeled Designer Drugs," Legal Newsline, January 9, 2013. http://legalnewsline.com.

70. Quoted in Governor Andrew M. Cuomo, "Governor Cuomo Launches Newest Phase of Statewide Campaign to Combat Synthetic Drugs and Prescription Drug Abuse," October 20, 2015. www.governor.ny.gov.

71. Quoted in Governor Andrew M. Cuomo, "Governor Cuomo Launches Newest Phase of Statewide Campaign to Combat Synthetic Drugs and Prescription Drug Abuse."

72. Quoted in Madison Mathews, "School Program Tackles Synthetic Drug Issue," *Johnson City (TN) Press*, March 14, 2012.

73. Quoted in Mathews, "School Program Tackles Synthetic Drug Issue."

74. Quoted in Mathews, "School Program Tackles Synthetic Drug Issue."

75. Quoted in Gus Burns, "Mayor Dave Bing Bans Sale of K2, Spice and Other Synthetic Marijuana in Detroit," MLive, June 5, 2012. www.mlive.com.

76. Quoted in Donna Leinwand Leger and Yasmeen Abutaleb, "Businesses Raided in Nationwide Crackdown on Synthetic Drugs," *USA Today*, July 25, 2012. http://usatoday30.usa today.com.

77. Quoted in *Convenience Store News*, "BP Latest Chain to Ban Sale of Spice and K2," June 6, 2012. www.csnews.com.

78. Quoted in *Milford (MA) Daily News*, "Attorney General Presses Gas Stations to Ban Synthetic Drugs," February 10, 2015. www.milforddailynews.com.

Community Anti-Drug Coalitions of America (CADCA)

625 Slaters Ln., Suite 300
Alexandria, VA 22314
phone: (800) 542-2322; fax: (703) 706-0565
e-mail: info@cadca.org • website: www.cadca.org

Representing more than five thousand community coalitions and affiliates, the CADCA seeks to make America's communities safe, healthy, and drug free. Its website offers policy information, news articles, and other information about many drugs, including synthetic drugs.

Drug Free America Foundation

5999 Central Ave., Suite 301
Saint Petersburg, FL 33710
phone: (727) 828-0211 • fax: (727) 828-0212
e-mail: webmaster@dfaf.org • website: www.dfaf.org

The Drug Free America Foundation is a drug prevention policy organization. Its website has news and articles about many drugs and prevention initiatives, including those focused on synthetic drugs.

Drug Policy Alliance

131 W. Thirty-Third St., 15th Floor
New York, NY 10001
phone: (212) 613-8020 • fax: (212) 613-8021
e-mail: nyc@drugpolicy.org • website: www.drugpolicy.org

The Drug Policy Alliance promotes alternatives to current drug policy that are grounded in science, compassion, health, and human rights. Its website features drug facts, statistics, information about drug laws, and articles about numerous drugs, including synthetics.

Foundation for a Drug-Free World

1626 N. Wilcox Ave., Suite 1297
Los Angeles, CA 90028
phone: (818) 952-5260; toll-free: (888) 668-6378
e-mail: info@drugfreeworld.org • website: www.drugfreeworld.org

The Foundation for a Drug-Free World provides information about drugs to youth and adults to help them make informed decisions and live drug free. A wealth of information is available on the interactive website, including articles specifically related to synthetic drug abuse.

National Institute on Drug Abuse (NIDA)

National Institutes of Health
6001 Executive Blvd., Room 5213
Bethesda, MD 20892-9561
phone: (301) 443-1124
e-mail: information@nida.nih.gov • website: www.drugabuse.gov

The NIDA supports research efforts that improve drug abuse prevention, treatment, and policy. The website links to a separate NIDA for Teens site, which is designed especially for young people and provides a wealth of information about drugs, including synthetic drugs.

Office of National Drug Control Policy

750 Seventeenth St. NW
Washington, DC 20503
phone: (800) 666-3332 • fax: (202) 395-6708
e-mail: ondcp@ncjrs.org • website: www.whitehouse.gov/ondcp

A component of the Executive Office of the President, the Office of National Drug Control Policy is responsible for directing the federal government's antidrug programs. A wide variety of publications can be found on the website.

Partnership for Drug-Free Kids

352 Park Ave. S., 9th Floor
New York, NY 10010
phone: (212) 922-1560 • fax: (212) 922-1570
website: www.drugfree.org

The Partnership for Drug-Free Kids is dedicated to helping parents and families solve the problem of teenage substance abuse. A large number of informative publications and current articles are available on its website.

Substance Abuse and Mental Health Services Administration (SAMHSA)

1 Choke Cherry Rd.
Rockville, MD 20857
phone: (877) 726-4727 • fax: (240) 221-4292
e-mail: samhsainfo@samhsa.hhs.gov • website: www.samhsa.gov

SAMHSA's mission is to reduce the impact of substance abuse and mental illness on America's communities. The site offers numerous articles, fact sheets, and other types of publications on drug-related topics.

To the Maximus Foundation

1120 Grenada Dr.
Aurora, IL 60506
phone: (630) 892-3629
e-mail: info@2themax.org • website: http://2themax.org

Created in the memory of a teen who died after using synthetic marijuana, the To the Maximus Foundation is committed to education and awareness of the dangers of synthetic drugs. Its website offers news releases, fact sheets, testimonials, links to other resources, and a blog.

US Drug Enforcement Administration (DEA)

8701 Morrissette Dr.
Springfield, VA 22152
phone: (202) 307-1000
website: www.dea.gov • teen website: www.justthinktwice.com

An agency of the US Department of Justice, the DEA is the United States' leading law enforcement agency for combating the sale and distribution of illegal drugs. Its website links to a separate teen site that provides a wealth of information about drugs, including synthetic drugs.

FOR FURTHER RESEARCH

Books

William Dudley, *Synthetic Drug Addiction*. San Diego, CA: ReferencePoint, 2015.

Peggy J. Parks, *Bath Salts and Other Synthetic Drugs*. San Diego, CA: ReferencePoint, 2013.

Peggy J. Parks, *How Serious a Problem Is Synthetic Drug Use?* San Diego, CA: ReferencePoint, 2015.

Mary E. Williams, *Synthetic Drugs*. Farmington Hills, MI: Greenhaven, 2014.

Internet Sources

Tricia Escobedo, "What You Need to Know About Synthetic Drugs," CNN, September 13, 2013. www.cnn.com/2013/09/13/health/synthetic-drugs-7-things.

Steve Featherstone, "Spike Nation," *New York Times*, July 8, 2015. www.nytimes.com/2015/07/12/magazine/spike-nation.html?_r=1.

Drew Griffin and Nelli Black, "Deadly High: How Synthetic Drugs Are Killing Kids," CNN, December 2, 2014. www.cnn.com/2014/12/01/us/synthetic-drugs-investigation.

Susan Donaldson James, "Flakka: New Synthetic Drug Is More Potent than Predecessors," NBC News, April 15, 2015. www.nbcnews.com/health/health-news/flakka-attack-new-synthetic-drug-joins-list-spanning-lsd-molly-n341506.

National Institute on Drug Abuse, "Emerging Trends," May 2015. www.drugabuse.gov/drugs-abuse/emerging-trends.

Stephen Stock and David Paredes, "The Law Has Trouble Keeping Up with Synthetic Drugs," NBC Bay Area, February 13, 2014. www.nbcbayarea.com/investigations/The-Law-Cant-Keep-Up -with-Synthetic-Drugs-244805391.html.

Websites

Above the Influence (http://abovetheinfluence.com). This website is a program of the Partnership for Drug-Free Kids and offers teens information about drugs and alcohol along with education about the influences that can pressure a teen to try drugs and alcohol, including fact pages about spice and bath salts.

Dirtiest Kept Secret (www.thedirtiestkeptsecret.org). An anti–synthetic drug website, run by parents who lost a son to synthetic drugs, that offers facts, news, and other education about synthetic drugs.

Just Think Twice (www.justthinktwice.com). An antidrug website that gives teens information, news, true stories, consequences, and facts about drugs and addiction, including synthetic drugs.

Know the Dangers (http://knowthedangers.com). A website sponsored by the Minnesota Department of Human Services that gives teens and parents information about synthetic drugs.

K2 Drug Facts (https://k2drugfacts.wordpress.com). This website provides teens with facts, news, information, and testimonials about synthetic marijuana.

INDEX

PICTURE CREDITS

ABOUT THE AUTHOR

Carla Mooney is the author of many books for young adults and children. She lives in Pittsburgh, Pennsylvania, with her husband and three children.